A Student's Guide to the
Internet

Carol Lea Clark
University of Texas at El Paso

Prentice Hall
Upper Saddle River, New Jersey 07458

Library of Congress Cataloging-in-Publication Data

Clark, Carol Lea.
    A student's guide to the Internet / Carol Lea Clark.
      p.   cm.
    Includes index.
    ISBN 0-13-442310-0
    1. Internet (Computer network)   2. Computer network resources.
I. Title.
TK5105.875.I57C53   1996
004.6'7—dc20   95–35805
                                               CIP

Acquisitions editor: Alison Reeves
Editorial/production supervision: Bruce Hobart/Pine Tree Composition, Inc.
Cover designer: Bruce Kenselaar
Editorial assistant: Kane Tung
Buyer: Mary Ann Gloriande

Acknowledgments

I would like to thank colleagues and friends who have encouraged and advised me during the writing of this book. These include G. Douglas Meyers, Carl Jackson, Evelyn Posey, Katherine Mangelsdorf, and Michael Kolitsky at the University of Texas at El Paso, as well as Alison Reeves and John Chillingworth at Prentice Hall. Others are Doreen Mowatt, Rose Usry, Morris Usry, Amber Lea Clark, and Ken Kenyon. I would also like to thank Joey Etheredge, my research assistant, for his invaluable help with technical issues and for lending his perspective as a writer and as a student.

Internet screen credits

CARL UnCover, the Carl Corporation Network; David W. Riggins, Gopher Jewels; Ken Schweller, CollegeTown; WAIS Inc.; Michael Hart, Project Gutenberg.

Printed in the United States of America
10 9 8 7 6 5 4 3 2 1

ISBN: 0-13-442310-0

Prentice-Hall International (UK) Limited, *London*
Prentice-Hall of Australia Pty. Limited, *Sydney*
Prentice-Hall Canada, Inc., *Toronto*
Prentice-Hall Hispanoamericana, S.A., *Mexico*
Prentice-Hall of India Private Limited, *New Delhi*
Prentice-Hall of Japan, Inc., *Tokyo*
Simon & Schuster Asia Pte. Ltd., *Singapore*
Editora Prentice-Hall do Brasil, Ltda., *Rio de Janeiro*

CONTENTS

9   File Transfer Protocol (FTP)   117

10   Telnet   144

PART ONE

INTRODUCTION

ONE

WHAT IS THE INTERNET?

THE INTERNET IS A WORLDWIDE NETWORK OF NETWORKS, connecting computers that range from simple desktop models to the largest and most sophisticated super computers. This web of computers is the core of the much talked about "Information Superhighway" and is rapidly changing the way that people around the world communicate with one another.

No one person or organization is in charge of the Internet. It is a collective effort, created and maintained by many thousands of individuals and organizations around the world. Because it is so large and complex, crossing national borders and intercontinental distances, the Internet offers people around the globe an opportunity to express ideas, voice opinions, and display creativity before a worldwide audience.

Your university probably has a computer network which professors, staff, and students use to process data and to store information. These same computers allow students and staff to communicate with each other and with thousands of other people around the world because in many cases these computers are not only connected to one another but are also part of a larger regional network. This regional network links your university's computer network to computer networks at nearby universities and may even link to networks belonging to local hobbyists or businesses. This regional network allows computers on your network to share information with the computers on those other networks. And the connections don't stop there.

The regional network is linked to other regional networks around the world. These connections span continents and oceans, making use of satellite connections and transoceanic cables to combine all of the regional networks into one network of networks, the Internet.

The network at your university is considered a *node*,* or location on the Internet. You might think of your node as a city on a world map. Each individual computer in the university network is a house in the city. Your network and many neighboring networks are linked together to form large regional networks, just as a group of cities make up a nation. If you have an electronic mailbox address on your university computer network, you can communicate with students in Germany, Russia, or South America just as easily as with students at your own university.

In some ways the Internet is like the telephone system. The international telephone system is composed of different telephone companies, some private and some governmental, all connected to each other. If you called a friend in Paris or New Delhi, you wouldn't need to know all the links connecting your telephone with your friend's. The different companies have established the links and found ways to make their technology compatible. The Internet community has also established links which allow a measure of compatibility between all of the local and regional networks.

The Internet is not new. Its beginnings date back to the 1960s, and it has been used for years by academics and scientists collaborating on research. These same individuals and others also discovered and expanded the Internet's potential for recreational use. Indeed, the Internet is one place where boundaries between professional and recreational use are blurred. Recently, Internet usage has spread to professionals in many fields who previously had used computers only for word processing or not at all. Also more and more students are discovering the professional, research, and recreational resources on the Internet. Experts estimate that there are more than 25 million users currently, and the number doubles every year.

WHY IS IT BECOMING SO POPULAR?

The Internet is the most comprehensive communication medium ever developed. With it an individual can easily communicate information quickly and relatively inexpensively to any number of people anywhere in the world. Through the Internet users can discuss issues and exchange ideas with hundreds, perhaps thousands, of people they have never met. The Internet can be used to view artwork, to listen to music, to access library catalogs and databases, to obtain software or electronic books, to get the latest satellite weather maps, and even to communicate with friends on the other side of the world. With the new developments of Internet video conferencing, real-time digital audio, and real-time Internet-wide document sharing, the list of potential uses is growing every day.

---

*A node, also called a host, is a computer on the Internet. This computer runs a program that accepts your connections and commands.

WHAT DOES THE INTERNET OFFER STUDENTS?

The Internet is changing the patterns of communication and research within universities. From a computer in an office, at home, or in a lab, professors—and students—can access faraway library catalogs, on-line reference books and journals, and databases. They can also join topical discussion groups and search through archives, thus keeping up to date on the latest thinking in their fields. The Internet is becoming an important component of classes in many different fields, with some classes even being held completely on-line.

The usefulness of the Internet does not end at graduation. The fastest growing sector of the Internet is corporate America, and Internet literacy is becoming increasingly important in many fields, including education, health care, and law.

BACKGROUND OF THE INTERNET

The Internet grew out of a project with grim intentions. During the late 1960s the U.S. Department of Defense began a project with a group known as the Advanced Research Projects Agency (ARPA). The people at ARPA were assigned to find ways of decentralizing computer communication so that, in the event of a nuclear attack, the United States would not be without computer communication links. Thus a network called ARPANET was established in 1969 for use by government and university researchers. The critical element in connecting the computers in ARPANET was finding a way for them to "talk" to each other. During the 1970s several *protocols,** or sets of rules for network communication, were tested and implemented, and in the process other networks were created by scientists and universities outside of ARPA. By the mid 1980s one of the protocols was chosen to link all of the networks. The solution was a protocol called TCP/IP (Transmission Control Protocol/ Internet Protocol).

TCP/IP sends information a little at a time by dividing the information into units called packets. These packets contain routing instructions explaining where the packet needs to go. The computers on each network interpret the instructions and send the packet onward toward its destination. A packet may pass through 30 or 40 computers before it arrives at its final destination. This system of routing allows the Internet to remain decentralized, which means that there is no one central location where all these packets of information have to go to be sorted and sent out, and if one *routing computer†* goes down, others will simply take over the work. The packets of information can take any of many routes to a destination, and, because they each contain information about where they are supposed to go, they rarely get lost, even in such a complex web of connections.

---

*A protocol is a set of agreed-upon rules detailing how to transmit data across a network or between networks.

†A routing computer processes packets of data and sends them on toward their destinations.

WHO PAYS FOR AND WHO CONTROLS THE INTERNET?

There is no central funding or governing body for the Internet. Each computer network system has its own funding and administrative procedures. Until fairly recently the Internet was primarily for research, educational, and private usage, and the National Science Foundation and the Internet Society exerted considerable authority over acceptable use of the Internet. More recently, especially in the World Wide Web, commercial usage has escalated rapidly. Today much of the day-to-day Internet policies are set by mutual agreement of users.

THE INTERNET IS UNDER CONSTRUCTION

The resources available on the Internet are extensive and compelling, but the Internet can be challenging to use because it is constantly under construction and many parts are subject to regular change. To make use of the Internet's power, you have to know how to locate the information you want and what commands are necessary to access that information. In fact, many new developments, such as the powerful facilities of the World Wide Web, have simplified the process considerably by providing a single front end through which you can do everything from browsing an FTP archive to posting USENET news. However, universal access to the World Wide Web is not yet a reality, and it is still important to understand how to use many of the older access methods or protocols. None of these protocols is really difficult; it just takes some time to learn which commands to use for each.

HOW CAN YOU LEARN ABOUT THE INTERNET?

A wealth of information about how to use the Internet exists on the Internet itself. But how do you learn how to find this information? It may seem you have to know how to navigate the Internet to learn how to navigate the Internet. Sound like a paradox? There are, of course, many guides to the Internet available at your local bookstore. There are are also many large directories available that give locations of interesting files and databases. The Internet is growing and changing so fast, however, that no printed guide can be complete and accurate. Discussion groups begin every day, and others are discontinued. Database sites continually add and delete files, change their directories, and develop connections to new sites. New protocols are developed for accessing information, and old ones become less useful.

Much of what is useful on the Internet can be discovered only by exploration, by trial-and-error application of the tools that are discussed in this book. Fortunately, the Internet is self-referential: you learn in a discussion group about a great new Web site, or vice versa. Or you may explore an archive looking for a specific file and find other information that is of even greater interest.

The way to learn about the Internet is to find a place to start and take time to investigate many of the fantastic resources it makes available. This book can be your entry point to the Internet and give you enough information to begin your explorations.

FIND A RESOURCE PERSON

No one book can tell you everything you need to know about the Internet. Many sources of on-line help, such as FAQs, or Frequently Asked Question lists (references maintained by many Internet sites and discussion groups), and Help-Net (a LISTSERV where users post their questions and then more experienced users post answers) are mentioned in this book. You also need to find one or more resource persons who can answer your questions. One may be your system administrator. Others may be in your university's computer labs or at the university computer help desk. Or you may find fellow students who are Internet explorers. Locate these people and nurture the connections because they can be of immense help to you.

ORGANIZATION OF THIS BOOK

Chapter 2 discusses ways to connect to the Internet, including through university mainframe computers and commercial providers. It is followed by chapters on communicating through electronic mail, LISTSERVs, USENET newsgroups, and real-time protocols such as CHAT and MUDs. The next portion concentrates on protocols for finding information on the Internet, such as the World Wide Web, gopher, and FTP. This portion ends with a chapter on hints for searching the Internet. Finally, a glossary defines words used in this book, and a bibliography suggests other books and Internet documents for those who want to learn more.

WELCOME TO THE INTERNET ADVENTURE

The Internet is more than anything else a state of mind. The Internet is a desire to cross boundaries of place and politics and to communicate with others. It is a quest for knowledge. The Internet is frustrating and exhilarating, rewarding and time consuming. The Internet is very much what you make of it. Welcome.

T W O

Getting Connected

IF YOU ARE A STUDENT IN A COLLEGE OR UNIVERSITY, chances are that you can get an electronic mail address through your school. Many schools offer their students electronic mail free or at low cost. Some universities limit access to students taking certain classes, while others provide wider access, sometimes even to surrounding community residents as well as students, faculty, and staff. Being able to connect to and explore the Internet through your university is an incredible benefit. Just a few years ago Internet access for those not involved in scientific or academic research was difficult to acquire.

In the previous chapter the Internet is compared to the worldwide telephone system with its seamless service network. The analogy breaks down, however, when the average individual tries to connect to the Internet. While telephones are common household items, Internet-connected computers are not. Unless you are part of a university or other institution with a direct connection to the Internet, you are forced to negotiate a sometimes bewildering array of providers that offer differing degrees of Internet connectivity for a fee.

Your university probably has a local computer network which is connected to the Internet via dedicated high-speed lines which provide continuous on-line access and, hopefully, a full range of Internet services including electronic mail and client/server programs. Client/server is a phrase you will run into several times in this book. It simply means that you as a user run "client" programs which request services from other computers on the Internet that are "servers," serving your requests, and you do this through the connection provided by your university's computer network.

Universities vary in the sophistication and scope of their computer networks, which can range from bare bones to state-of-the-art equipment and software. They also vary in the kinds of connections they offer to students. Some universities offer a number of access options, and others may offer only one or two. Following are several typical configurations.

TYPES OF CONNECTIONS

1. *Terminal Access.* Most universities have at least one powerful computer connected directly to the Internet and shared by members of the faculty, staff, and student body. This type of computer, which may vary from an older mainframe design to a fast modern workstation, has one universal trait: a multi-user operating system. This system, also known as a time-sharing system, is different from a desktop computer in that it can be used by many people at once. The processing power of the machine is shared among all of the users, hence the name "time-sharing system."

The most basic form of Internet access is through a terminal connected to a time-sharing system. A typical terminal consists of a monitor and a keyboard which are connected to the system. One time-sharing system may have hundreds of terminals or just a few, and the actual time-sharing computer may not even be in the same building as the terminals.

You may have worked with this type of system before. Many large public libraries offer their card catalogs via computer terminals. You can interact with the card-catalog computer, submitting searches by author, subject, or title. Usually there are several terminals available to search from, and those terminals are all connected to the library's main computer.

Universities that offer this type of Internet connection usually have a computer lab or labs where many terminals are located. All you need to do is obtain permission to use the lab and learn how to use the time-sharing system.

Time-sharing networks may provide a *shell* system of menu screens which offer options to the user. They are called "shell" systems because they run as a shell around the basic operations of the system. Or, instead of menus, they may have a "naked" prompt or command line requiring the user to know specific commands.

2. *Dial-in Terminal Emulation.* A university offering a time-sharing system may allow users to connect from home via dial-in access. Once connected, the home computer acts as a terminal on the network, just as if it were a computer in one of the on-campus labs. The programs run on the system computer, not on the computer you are using. Thus once you access the network, it does not matter whether you are using an IBM-compatible or Macintosh; the commands are the same. Dial-in terminal emulation requires that your computer have a modem. You will also need a piece of software called a terminal emulator which allows a computer to mimic a terminal on a computer system. Usually the university will either provide a terminal emulator or recommend one for you to use. With this type of connection, you can transfer files across the Internet only to and from the system computer, not to and from your computer. Therefore, you must use a separate procedure to move files between the system computer and your own. Many terminal emulators have file trans-

fer procedures built in. Finally, when you are using this type of connection, you are limited by the speed of both your university's system and your own modem, so you may have to be patient when attempting a detailed operation.

3. *Network Connection.* If your university has invested in a modern network-based computer lab facility, you may find fast and friendly Internet access much easier to obtain. Internet programs such as Pine Mail, Fetch (FTP), WinGopher, and Mosaic may be offered as point-and-click options on computers in labs. These are powerful, user-friendly versions of the major Internet programs and allow files to be downloaded directly to a computer disk. Computers using this type of connection are usually connected to a local area network, based on one of many high-speed networking protocols, such as Ethernet or Token-Ring. This local network is connected directly to the Internet through a gateway that converts from the network protocol to TCP/IP, the protocol that the Internet uses. This is one of the fastest and most versatile ways to make use of Internet resources.

4. *Dial-in Network Connection.* SLIP (Serial Line Internet Protocol) or PPP (Point-to-Point) connections allow the user to install and operate Internet programs on a home computer, accessing the university's system via modem and using it as a point of entry to the Internet. These connections, which require an account on the university's system, offer the most flexibility and individual control but are not available at all universities. Some universities that offer SLIP or PPP provide software to students, along with instructions on how to install and operate it. To take full advantage of SLIP or PPP connections, you will need a fairly sophisticated computer and a relatively fast modem, with a minimum of 9600 bps. A central computer at the university acts as a gateway between the SLIP or PPP protocol and TCP/IP.

Dial-in network connections work much the same way that network connections do. You can use the same user-friendly programs you would in a network connection; and, because the programs are located on your computer, you have even more control.

An additional advantage of SLIP or PPP connections is that they may allow you to perform multiple tasks at the same time. You could, for example, run an Archie search (see Chapter 9) in one window and, while you are waiting, read your electronic mail in another window.

UNIVERSITY OPERATING SYSTEMS

Systems such as UNIX, VMS, and CMS are used to operate the powerful time-sharing workstations that provide access to the Internet. These systems manage computer resources in much the same way that DOS manages the operations of an IBM compatible PC. The chief advantage of these workstation operating systems is their ability to manage many system operations simultaneously, allowing a number of individuals to use the same workstation at once. Because there are several different operating systems, the commands to access Internet protocols will vary according to the system being used. For example, to list the contents of a directory in DOS, the command is **dir;** in UNIX, however, the command is **ls.**

NON-UNIVERSITY CONNECTIONS

Even if you are able to secure an Internet connection through your university, you should be aware of some of the other types of connections available. You will not, after all, be a student forever (hopefully) and may want to continue your Internet explorations after your student days. Alternatively, you may not be satisfied with the level of connectivity your university provides and may decide to explore other options to augment their services.

Non-university connections include free-nets and various commercial providers of different kinds and levels of connectivity.

1. *Free-Nets.* If you happen to live in an area serviced by a free-net, you may want to explore its services. Free-nets are community computing networks established to broaden access to computer networking. Many were originally computer bulletin boards but have broadened their services to feature Internet connections. They may offer interesting connections and databases, as well as electronic mail. You can also explore out-of-area free-nets via Telnet.

2. *Commercial Providers.* Commercial on-line providers such as America Online (AOL), CompuServe, Delphi, and Prodigy began as bulletin board and reference services but they have expanded to offer a user-friendly interface to the Internet and many of its services. They provide other services such as full-text magazine and newspaper articles, on-line homework help, and specialized discussion forums. If your university does not offer a dial-up connection to the Internet that you can access from home, you may want to consider subscribing to one of the major commercial providers so that you can connect to the Internet from your home computer. Even if your university does offer dial-up connection, you may want to consider using one of the commercial providers as an auxiliary source of information.

All offer discussion groups (often called forums) on computer-related topics such as desktop publishing and software packages. CompuServe, for example, has more than 700 forums, including ones on professional topics such as aviation, entrepreneurs, business, investing, journalism, public relations, marketing, and working from home.

CompuServe's on-line library includes an electronic version of the *Academic American Encyclopedia* and *Grolier's Encyclopedia.* On-line versions of magazines include *Consumer Reports, U.S. News and World Report,* and *PC World.* CompuServe's Executive News Services monitors the *Washington Post* and wire services such as the Associated Press, United Press International, and Reuters for current news and business features. The Newspaper Archives is a searchable database for more than 50 U.S. and British newspapers.

America Online's magazines include *Consumer Reports, Omni,* the *Atlantic Monthly,* the *New Republic, Saturday Review, Time Magazine,* and *Wired.* Newspapers include the *New York Times, Chicago Tribune,* and the *San Jose Mercury.* Reuters, CNN, and UPI provide additional current news coverage.

Offerings for the other commercial on-line services are similar, and all continually expand and update their offerings. At publication time all offered limited Internet access including e-mail, and several were expanding to near-complete access.

Costs for commercial providers begin at about $10 a month for a minimum number of hours, with charges for extra hours and sometimes for premium services.

3. *Internet Service Providers*. These local or regional providers are appearing with increasing frequency, offering a widely varying degree of Internet services and prices. Many are time-sharing systems, but an increasing number offer PPP and SLIP connections.

Costs for access to the Internet via an Internet service provider vary from a flat monthly fee of about $10 to a $10 per hour charge; the average is $20 to $25 a month for 20 hours. If your university does not offer full Internet access and you are in an area without a local service provider, you may want to check out those with national 800 numbers, although they pass on the long-distance charge of $5 to $8 an hour to you.

HOW CONNECTED IS YOUR CONNECTION?

Not all computers connected to the Internet are actually "on" the Internet. While this may sound confusing, it is quite true. You already know that there are millions of computers out there acting as active parts of the Internet, whether a powerful workstation managing a large public access database, or a network-connected PC. Part or all of the processing power of these machines is dedicated to running Internet protocols. The giant database manager may process thousands of requests each day and is obviously part of the Internet; the network-connected PC may do little more than run software that provides easy access to Internet protocols (such as a news reader or a Gopher client), but it is also a part of the Internet. So that means that all computers that can access the Internet are a part of the Internet, right? Not really.

There is one major difference between having access to the Internet and being a part of the Internet. The difference lies in how involved a computer is in the actual processing of Internet information. Many universities support home dial-up access to time-sharing systems. You simply need a home computer and a modem. Once connected, you may be working from a command prompt or an easy-to-use menu system. You may be able to create e-mail or access a newsgroup. This does not mean that your computer is a part of the Internet. It is simply working as a terminal connected to the time-sharing system (the software for this type of connection is called a terminal emulator because it allows your computer to emulate a display terminal wired directly to the time-sharing system). How is this different from a networked PC? The network-connected PC is able to send mail, transfer files, or connect to go-pher sites without first contacting the time-sharing system; it does all of those things itself. In contrast, a computer connected as a terminal simply re-lays commands to the time-sharing system and displays the time-sharing system's responses; the terminal does not actually carry out the instructions itself.

There are a few cases where the distinction may seem to blur. SLIP and PPP connections dial in to a time-sharing server via a modem, just like a con-nection through a terminal emulator. There are also some advanced terminal emulator programs, such as Kermit that allow files to be transferred from a time-sharing system to a personal computer. While not quite as obvious, the distinction still applies. SLIP and PPP connections are really just network con-nections, modified to work over a phone line. From the time you dial in until the time you disconnect, your personal computer is truly a part (although one of the slower parts) of the Internet. Advanced terminal emulators, even those providing basic file transfer abilities, are still terminal emulators. All of the ac-tual Internet protocols and client operations remain in the hands of the time-sharing system that they are connected to.

There is one last, important distinction between computers that are ac-tually on the Internet and those that just access it. Every computer that is part of the Internet has an Internet address. Terminals don't have addresses, but the systems that they connect to do. SLIP, PPP and network-linked comput-ers have Internet addresses. No two computers connected to the Internet will use the same address simultaneously. Addresses for SLIP and PPP connec-tions may change slightly every time you connect, but you will never use the same address that someone else is using.

WHAT CONNECTIONS DOES YOUR UNIVERSITY OFFER?

Universities are anything but consistent in the Internet services they offer and the ways users can access those services. The only way to find out is to ask. Your uni-versity's computer help desk or system administrator can provide you with basic information and tell you where to turn for more. Many universities offer free or low-cost seminars about the Internet to students and most provide handouts or have on-line manuals. Don't be discouraged if you have to ask several people to find answers to your questions. Internet usage is expanding so quickly that many universities are still adjusting to the demand. Be persistent. The wealth of informa-tion on the Internet is worth the time and trouble you will invest in learning how to access it.

QUESTIONS TO ASK

1. What type of Internet access does your university offer students? A menu-driven shell system? SLIP or PPP? Something else?
2. What type of system or systems are offered (UNIX, VMS, CMS, etc.)?
3. Does the university offer Internet training seminars?
4. Are there on-line manuals? How do you access them? Are there handouts?
5. Does your university system support dial-up access?
   - If so, are you offered a shell account on a time-sharing system, or SLIP or PPP access, or a choice?
   - What modem speed will the university system support?
   - How do you set up your modem and software? What phone number do you need to dial?
6. If your university offers SLIP or PPP connections, does it provide software? If not, does it offer suggestions on what software to use?
7. If your university does not provide full Internet access (including USENET and World Wide Web, for example), are there local providers who do, and what do they cost?
8. If your university does not offer SLIP or PPP connections, are there local providers who do, and what do they cost?
9. Does your university have a lab of network-connected computers? If so, are they available for all students to use or are they limited to certain classes or departments? What are the lab hours?

PART TWO

COMMUNICATING WITH OTHERS

T H R E E

ELECTRONIC MAIL

ELECTRONIC MAIL, commonly called e-mail, refers to messages sent electronically from one computer user to another. It is by far the most popular service on the Internet. Many who regularly use e-mail never take advantage of the rich resources available through other Internet protocols, viewing the Internet simply as a cheap and easy way to send messages to friends and colleagues. Others find that e-mail is an easy initiation to the Internet. It is a tool they can use to learn more about how and where to travel on the information superhighway.

E-mail is fast. Messages are often transmitted almost instantaneously, and even if there is a backlog in the sender's or receiver's system, messages usually arrive within a day. Users of e-mail often disparagingly refer to the mail carried by the postal service as "snail mail."

E-mail is cheap. Once you are connected to a network, e-mail is usually free or low cost. It is almost always cheaper than a stamp and envelope or the price of a long-distance phone call. There is no special charge for speedy delivery or international mail.

E-mail is convenient. You can write and send e-mail messages any time you like without worrying about penmanship or whether you have any stamps. With e-mail you can whip off a quick note to anyone at three o'clock in the morning without waking the person up with the telephone. Messages sit in the recipient's mailbox until he or she has time to read them. What is most appealing to many, though, is the special nature of electronic mail communication. E-mail is somehow both more immediate and more casual than is a traditional letter; people who have never met correspond comfortably via electronic mail about common interests when they might not so readily converse via telephone or conventional mail.

Increasingly, e-mail is becoming a universal medium of communication. More and more networks, including commercial ones such as America Online and Delphi, are connecting to the Internet. You can easily communicate with users of another system; you only need to know the correct addresses.

Electronic mail is not a perfect replacement for a phone call. Your correspondent can't hear variations in the intonation of your voice. The casualness of e-mail is often deceiving. People may write comments they intend to be humorous or

---

SIGNATURES AND SMILIES

As e-mail has evolved, a couple of interesting conventions have been adopted to address some of the quirks of the system. The most common of these conventions are signatures and smilies.

During the late 1970s and early 1980s many of the major networks that today make up important parts of the Internet were still separated by minor variations in how they communicated. Sending an e-mail message between computers connected to two different networks often resulted in part of the message being lost. More often than not it was the last few lines of a message that would disappear in the shuffle. In order to solve this dilemma, many people began to add signature lines to the end of their e-mail messages, consisting of an interesting quote or humorous statement, which added a certain amount of personality to a message. If the last few lines of a message were cut off, all that would be lost was the signature, and the mail would arrive just fine. During the last few years better standards for translation and inter-network communication have been established and accidental trimming has become rare. However, the tradition of adding an interesting signature has outlived its original purpose and become an art form all its own.

Smilies were created to compensate for the inability to express tone in e-mail. The complaint was that e-mail, unlike a telephone call, often did not accurately reflect the intonation intended by the sender. A sarcastic message could be misinterpreted as serious. Smilies were created to add the missing vocal inflection. You read a smilie by looking at the screen sideways, viewing the left of the screen as the top. The most basic smilie is :-). If you turn your head sideways, you can make out the cute smilie face. This smilie is used to denote a joking or sarcastic statement. Over the years, hundreds of smilies have come into being. Here are a few of the more common ones:

;-)   Winking smilie
:-(Frowning smilie
~:-(Angry smilie
(-:   Left-handed smilie

ironic, and their words may be misunderstood by the recipient who interprets them as serious or sarcastic. Veterans of e-mail manage to enliven their messages with customized signatures and smilies, or expressions created with text characters.

DEFINING ELECTRONIC MAIL

E-mail, put simply, is a message sent to another computer user electronically. You type the message in a mail program, text editor, or word processor and, instead of printing it out and putting it in an envelope, you dispatch it electronically to someone's e-mail mailbox.

Unlike paper mail, one piece of electronic mail is not limited to one recipient. One e-mail message can be sent from one person to many. You can create your own mailing lists of friends or colleagues. Or you can join discussion groups and communicate with people of common interests through e-mail (as you will see in Chapter 4).

E-mail messages consist of two basic parts: the control information and the content of the message. In Internet language the control information is called the header. It includes the sender's address, routing information, and the recipient's address. The content is the text of the message.

WHAT ARE INTERNET ADDRESSES?

Internet addresses are similar to phone numbers. If you are in Berlin and you want to call a friend in Los Angeles, you will use several levels of numbers to make the connection. You would begin by dialing the international number to reach the U.S. telephone system. Then you would need to dial the area code for Los Angeles. Now let's say your friend works in the regional sales office of a large motorcycle company which has a PBX switchboard. You would dial the seven-digit local number that would connect you to the PBX. You would then need to dial an extension to reach your friend. That is quite a few numbers, but if you pushed them all in the right order, the phone in your friend's office would ring.

Internet addresses are very similar. They are made up of several levels of numbers, and each level describes part of the location of the receiver's computer. Typical addresses contain three or four sets of numbers separated by periods (e.g., 128.83.128.230). The Internet address is used with a number of protocols, but the purpose is always the same: to locate the machine you wish to contact. You might Telnet to an Internet address, or run a gopher session with a machine accessed through its Internet address. And, of course, you can send e-mail to someone at an Internet address (someone@128.83.128.230).

But if you have seen e-mail addresses, you know that they are not usually made up of a bunch of numbers. They should look more like **someone@ marsala.xoflet.edu,** right? In fact, Internet addresses are rarely used directly with any protocol, be it e-mail, Telnet, gopher, or whatever. Instead, we use host names which are unique names with equivalent Internet addresses. They are simple to remember because they usually describe the host that they point to. The host name **bongo.cc.utexas.edu** refers to a computer named bongo at the computation center (cc) at the University of Texas (utexas), which is an educational site (edu). This is much easier to remember than **128.83.186.13,** which is the numeric equivalent for bongo's host name.

Host names (or addresses) consist of a local host name (made up of the machine name and the site name) and a domain name. Machine names are generally drawn from mythological references, cartoon characters, animal names, or allusions to sci fi or fantasy literature. In the example above the machine is named "bongo." Clusters of machines at the same site are often given names that relate to one another, such as red, blue, and green, or sleepy, dopey, and doc. The site name **cc.utexas** tells us where bongo is located: the University of Texas. What part of the University of Texas? The computation center. A suffix or extension following the host name is the domain name. Some important domains types are: **.com** (commercial), **.edu** (educational, mostly U.S.), **.net** (network operations), **.gov** (U.S. government), **.mil** (U.S. military), and **.org** (nonprofit organization). Most countries also have a domain. For example, **.us** (United States), **.uk** (United Kingdom), **.su** (ex-Soviet Union), **.au** (Australia), and **.fi** (Finland). Within the **.us** domain there are subdomains for all fifty states, each generally with a name identical to the state's postal abbreviation (although the domain for U.S and state are often omitted). Within the **.uk** domain there is an **.ac** subdomain for academic sites and a **.co** domain for commercial ones. Other top-level domains may be divided in similar ways.

When you use a host address, your system asks a special database or set of databases for the Internet numerical address of the host you wish to contact. Everything is actually done via the Internet numeric address, but you rarely have to think about this because the change from host name to Internet address is made transparent to you. You just have to remember the host name. . . most of the time. There are occasions when it becomes necessary to use the Internet address directly rather than the host name. When you use a host name, the system contacts a database called the Network Information Service, or a set of databases called the Domain Name Service to obtain the numeric equivalent of the host name. Major Internet sites around the world maintain copies of these databases and update them regularly. If a site is very new, the host name may not yet be listed in the database. The Internet numeric address will work, but the host name won't begin to work until the database is updated. As a general rule, if a host name does not seem to work, you can try the Internet address as a second option.

A Typical Internet Address

Let's look at a typical Internet e-mail address:

    JohnSmith@candy.usw.edu

Reading the address from left to right, **JohnSmith** is the name of the user. This is usually a first name, last name, initials, or a nickname. However, some sites issue user numbers rather than names, so this part of the address may be composed of arbitrary letters and numbers rather than a recognizable part of a name. The user name is followed by the **@** symbol, which is followed by **candy,** the name of the computer that receives JohnSmith's mail. Next is **usw,** the host name of the university where the computer "candy" is located. The last part of the address is the domain name **edu,** which tells you that "usw" is an educationally oriented site (a university). Other addresses may be longer, because of a lengthy host name or complex user name, but the logic of the parts remains the same.

Non-Internet Addresses

As was mentioned earlier, many networks are now connected to the Internet. Users of these other networks may have addresses structured differently from Internet addresses, but they can usually be used just like a regular Internet address. If you have difficulty sending mail to a user on a non-Internet network, consult your system administrator and on-line help documentation for aid in formatting an address that will work. Below are some examples that you can use to format some of the more common non-Internet addresses:

CompuServe	`UserNumber@compuserve.com`
America Online	`UserName@aol.com`
Prodigy	`UserID@prodigy.com`
GEnie	`UserID@genie.geis.com`
Delphi	`UserName@delphi.com`
Applelink	`UserName@applelink.apple.com`
AT&T Mail	`UserName@attmail.att.com`
MCI Mail	`UserID@mcimail.com`
BIX	`UserID@dcibix.das.net`
Bitnet	`UserName@site.bitnet`
FidoNet	`Firstname.Lastname@p4.f3.n2.z1.FidoNet.Org`

ELECTRONIC MAIL PROGRAMS

There is no one mail program that works on all systems. Conversely, you don't need to be using the same mail program as your recipient in order to have your messages received and read. If you have a PPP or SLIP connection with your university, allowing you to install Internet programs on your home computer, you will be able to choose from a number of mail programs. Otherwise, you will have to use the mail program or programs provided by your university computer network. All e-mail programs generally have the same or similar functions, but they use different commands for these functions.

Most mail programs will allow you to do the following:

1. Access and read your incoming mail
2. Save incoming mail in a file
3. Print incoming mail

4. Create and send new messages
5. Reply to a message
6. Forward a message to another user
7. Attach text or other type files into your mail messages

The ease with which these functions are possible varies widely from one program to another.

This chapter will demonstrate Pine and Eudora, two common and fairly user-friendly programs. If you don't have one of these programs, or even if you do and want to acquire a deeper knowledge of it, ask your system administrator or help desk staff. There are usually manuals available, often on-line, and many universities offer training classes for e-mail.

ACCESSING A MAIL PROGRAM

Most university computer networks allow you to access a mail program through one of three methods.

- If you have a window-oriented system, click on the icon of the mail program.
- If you have a command prompt, issue a command such as "mail."
- If you have a shell program, select "mail" from a menu.

If your university offers PPP or SLIP connections, you will be able to install a mail program on your home computer and typically will activate it by using the mouse to click on the program's icon.

You will need to ask your help desk assistant or system administrator how to access the mail program or programs at your university.

PINE DEMONSTRATION

Designed to be user friendly, Pine has a hot-key menu system. The main menu, reproduced below, for example, offers a selection of seven commands: help, compose message, folder index, folder list, address book, setup, and quit. Type the hot-key command or use up and down arrow keys to move highlighting on the menu until the command you want is indicated, and then press <ENTER>.

One of Pine's strongest features is its folder system. Three default folders are automatically created: INBOX (to store incoming e-mail), sent-mail (to store mail you have sent), and saved messages (where you can save incoming messages). You can add folders at any time by using the list command (l), then choosing (a) for add. Pine has a useful address book which allows you to create nicknames for addresses you want to have easily available. The program also includes a basic spell check; and it supports MIME, which means that you can attach nontext files such as software or image files to messages for transmission.

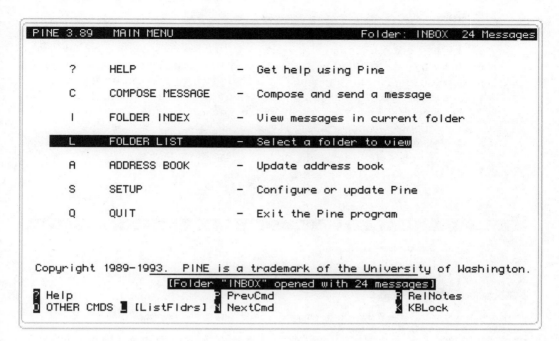

```
PINE 3.89    MAIN MENU                          Folder: INBOX   24 Messages

        ?      HELP              -  Get help using Pine

        C      COMPOSE MESSAGE   -  Compose and send a message

        I      FOLDER INDEX      -  View messages in current folder

        L      FOLDER LIST       -  Select a folder to view

        A      ADDRESS BOOK      -  Update address book

        S      SETUP             -  Configure or update Pine

        Q      QUIT              -  Exit the Pine program



Copyright 1989-1993.  PINE is a trademark of the University of Washington.
                 [Folder "INBOX" opened with 24 messages]
? Help                         P PrevCmd                      R RelNotes
O OTHER CMDS   [ListFldrs]  N NextCmd                      K KBLock
```

Sending Mail in Pine

Choose the "Compose Message" option from the main menu, and you will receive the template shown below.

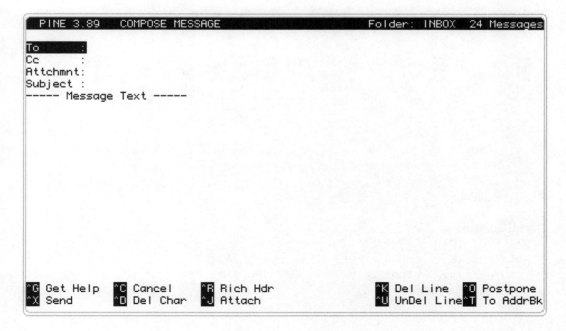

```
PINE 3.89    COMPOSE MESSAGE                    Folder: INBOX   24 Messages
To      :
Cc      :
Attchmnt:
Subject :
----- Message Text -----















^G Get Help   ^C Cancel     ^R Rich Hdr           ^K Del Line   ^O Postpone
^X Send       ^D Del Char   ^J Attach             ^U UnDel Line ^T To AddrBk
```

At the upper left of the screen you have spaces for "To," where you fill in the address of the person to whom you are writing; "Cc," which stands for carbon copy and allows you to fill in addresses, separated by commas, of other people whom you would like to receive the letter; "Attchmnt," where you can list the name of a MIME (nontext) file that you would like to send with the letter; and "Subject" for a brief message describing the contents of the letter. Across the bottom of the screen are menu options, including "Cancel" (for cancel message) and "Send."

The sample below shows a message composed with Pine and addressed to your friend and mine, John Smith.

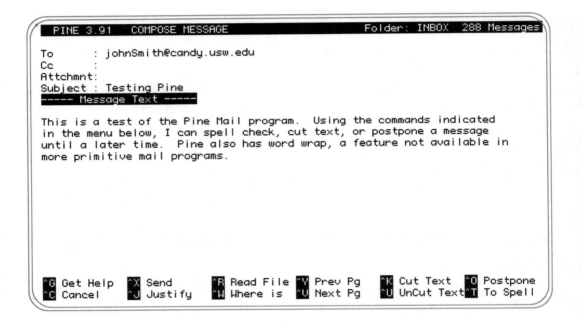

Note that the menu items in this screen vary from those in the previous screen. Pine alters its menus to offer different options based on your point in the message preparation process. Some screens also offer you an "O" menu option for other commands.

Reading Mail in Pine

To read mail, return to the main menu and select "Folder List". One of the default folders already created in Pine is INBOX, where new mail is posted. Highlight INBOX and press <ENTER>.

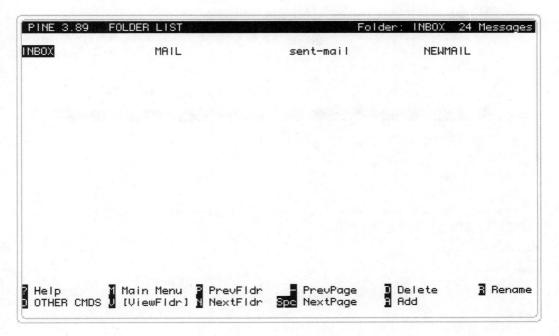

Select the INBOX option from the folder list menu to receive a list of your new mail.

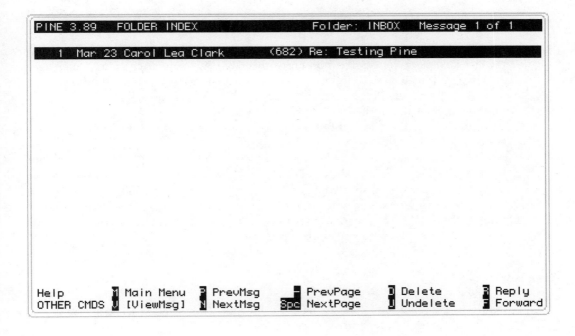

The letter below is an example of a message you would receive with Pine. From the content of the message, you can assume that it was created with a program other than Pine. Note the time and date stamped along with the address of the sender at the top of the letter.

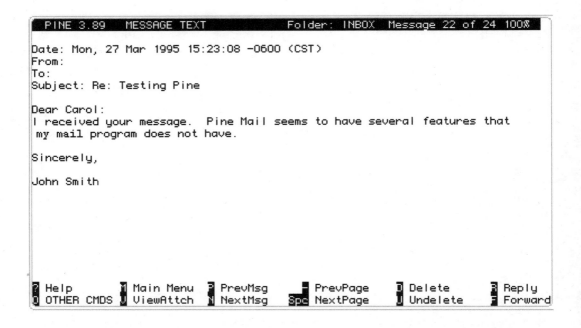

Should you want to reply to a message, you would select the "R" option from the hot-key menu across the bottom of the page. When you reply to a message, Pine will automatically fill in the subject line with **Re:(subject),** taking the subject from the subject line of the original message. Pine will also add the text of the original message at the end of the reply, indicated by a border of > marks. You can leave this echoed text to clarify your reply, or you can delete it by using the "^K" command to cut text.

Pine has a fairly good help system which explains some of the more intricate functions of the program. Also, under the "O" command (for other) in the "create mail" screen, there is a print command. Depending upon the configuration of Pine set up by your university, you may be able to print directly to your computer's printer. If this does not work, you will need to ask your help desk or system administrator to explain the appropriate procedure.

Closing Pine

Return to the main menu and choose "Q" for quit. The program will ask you if you really want to quit Pine, and you answer **y** for yes.

EUDORA DEMONSTRATION

Eudora is an attractive, point-and-click mail program, but you can use it only if you have a PPP or SLIP connection or a direct connection in a university network (usually in a lab). Eudora runs on your personal computer and comes in both Windows and Macintosh versions. An early version of Eudora is free, and later versions (with improvements) are sold commercially.

Eudora contacts your mail server at intervals you specify and checks to see whether new mail has arrived. If it has, it retrieves it to your computer and notifies you. Eudora has many attractive mailbox management features, including the capability to sort both incoming and outgoing mail into different mailboxes based on content. In the address book, you can specify nicknames for addressees, and Eudora will recognize them when you type them in the address space of a new message.

The following demonstration is the Macintosh version of Eudora; the Windows version is similar.

Sending Mail in Eudora

Go to **Message** in the menu bar across the top of the screen (above the window reproduced below) and select **New Message.** You will be given a template, like the one below, where you can fill in the address and the subject line. Your return address is automatically reproduced for you. Then you can compose your message in the space below the dotted line. Eudora will automatically word wrap unless you turn off the option by clicking on the fourth icon at the top of the page (the one with the page and the arrow).

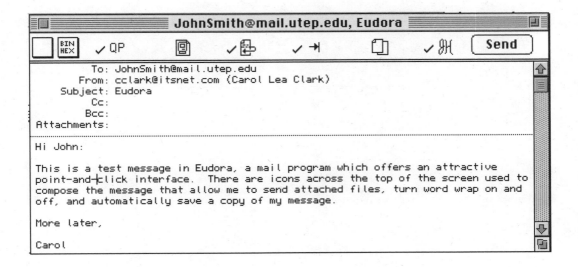

Reading Mail in Eudora

Under **File** in the menu bar across the top of the screen, select the **Check Mail** option, and you will see a spread-sheet-like list of columns with one line of status information for each message. An example follows:

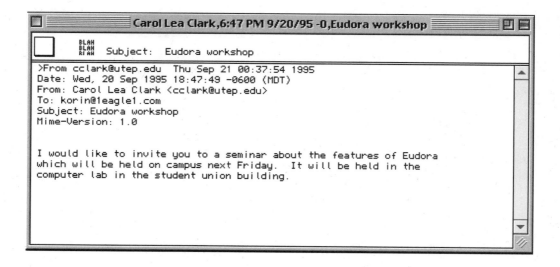

In the left-hand column are symbols indicating information about each piece of mail. The messages in the sample screen above have a ●. That means they have not been read. If this space is blank, that means the message has been read. An **R** indicates you have replied to the message, and **F** means the message has been forwarded. The address of the sender appears in the second column to the left, followed by the time and date the message was sent. The last column lists the subject line of the message.

Use the arrow keys to move the highlighting to the message which interests you, and press <ENTER> to read the mail message. The following letter repeats the address, date, and subject line information before giving the text of the message.

If you want to save or print this message, go to **File** on the menu bar and select the option you desire. To close this message, as with most Macintosh applications, click on the small box in the upper left-hand corner. If you want to delete the message, highlight it in the box which lists mail messages, and touch your delete key. The deleted message will go to the trash and will not be finally deleted until you empty the trash.

Creating Mailboxes

Eudora allows you to create mailboxes to organize your incoming messages. Simply choose the **Mailboxes** option under **Windows** in the menu bar at the top of your screen. You will receive a dialogue box allowing you to create mailboxes, change names of mailboxes, and create folders in which you can place several different mailboxes. The dialogue box looks like this:

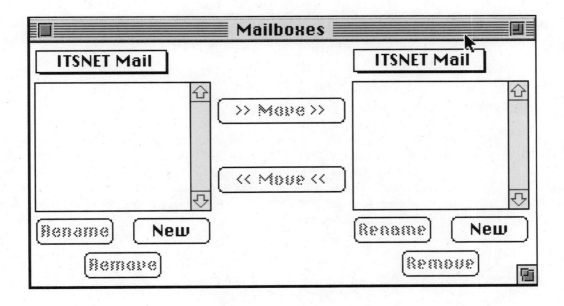

The ITSNET Mail headings refer to the server which provides this particular connection. You will have different headings in those spaces. To create mailboxes, click on the **New** button and another dialogue box will appear which asks you for the name of the mailbox. To move a piece of mail from one mailbox to another, go to **Transfer** in the menu bar.

Other Eudora Features

With Eudora, you can download your mail into your computer from the network, sever the connection, process your mail, and reconnect only to send new mail. This capability is an advantage when you are paying for connection time. Eudora is also one of the programs that most easily supports MIME functionality; that is, you can attach multiple files and binary data to your mail messages. The freeware version of Eudora used by many academic institutions may not offer some advanced features such as spell check which the commercial version offers. The spell check limitation, however, can be bypassed by composing messages in your word processing program and copying the complete spell-checked message into Eudora.

ASSIGNMENTS

1. Obtain a mailbox or account on your university's computer network. Find out what mail program or programs are available and whether there are any on-line manuals or printed instructions. Discuss what you have learned with your small group.
2. Analyze your mailbox address, locating your personal designation (whether abbreviated name or arbitrary letters and numbers), the name of the mail server machine, designation for your university site, domain name, and any other parts of the address.
3. Send a test e-mail message to a classmate.
4. As directed, reply to an e-mail message.

QUESTIONS TO ASK

1. How do you obtain an electronic mailbox address or account on the university's computer network? What are the terms? Is it free, or are you charged?
2. What mail program or programs are available? Are there on-line or printed manuals? Are there training sessions for e-mail?
3. If your university offers SLIP or PPP access, is a mail program made available to you for installation on your home computer?

LISTSERV: Internet Discussion Groups

WHAT ARE LISTSERVs?

LISTSERV consists of topic-oriented forums in which discussions are distributed by electronic mail. Topics range from accounting to zoology, and all that is required to participate is access to electronic mail and knowledge of a few basic commands. Any member of a LISTSERV can contribute a message.

There are two basic types of LISTSERV: moderated and unmoderated. In moderated groups all postings are sent to the LISTSERV, where they are collected, read, and either accepted or rejected. The postings are then usually assembled into a digest and are sent to all the members of the list. Digests, much like magazine issues, come out on a regular basis, usually biweekly or monthly.

Unmoderated groups simply transmit messages as they are received. This format allows users to hold conversations by posting back and forth to one another. This type of group tends to create a sense of community but has the drawback of generating a large amount of mail.

Although a simple concept, LISTSERV is among the most powerful tools on the Internet. Via LISTSERVs individuals can communicate personally with hundreds or thousands of people.

A WORD OR TWO ABOUT BITNET

LISTSERV lists were first developed for Bitnet, a large network developed in the mid-1980s to connect teachers and students around the world. The Bitnet network uses a different set of protocols than does the Internet. One of the differences is in the way that Bitnet handles e-mail. Bitnet addresses will not work properly on the Internet. As a result, LISTSERV groups were originally limited to Bitnet users. However, within the last few years most LISTSERV servers have begun to use gateways which allow them to communicate with people on the Internet. Likewise, many Internet sites have installed gateways (communications software that enable data to pass between dissimilar networks) that give users the ability to send mail to Bitnet, and thus to the LISTSERV goups. Many LISTSERV lists have also set up equivalent Internet e-mail addresses, which are not a part of Bitnet and so do not pose compatibility problems. It is usually safe to use the LISTSERVs that offer an Internet e-mail address, but special formatting may be required to send mail to someone with a Bitnet address. If you have trouble contacting a LISTSERV at its published address or addresses, ask your system administrator for advice.

HOW DO YOU SUBSCRIBE?

If you know how to use electronic mail, you already know most of what you need to know to join a LISTSERV list. You subscribe by sending mail to the LISTSERV server requesting that you be added to the mailing list. What is the LISTSERV server? It is a computer running a program that coordinates one or more lists. The volume of mail received by most LISTSERVs would overwhelm a human list manager, so lists are automated, programmed to respond in certain ways to specific commands. There are actually several different programs that manage lists, such as REVISED LISTSERV, Mailbase, Mailserv, and Unix ListProcessor (Listproc). This may sound complicated, but it is not. All these programs use similar commands, which are simple and straightforward.

The LISTSERV subscription process is quite simple. You send a message to the LISTSERV address with a subscription command as the text of the message. If you subscribe to CAMPCLIM, a forum for discussion pertaining to college environments, for instance, you would send mail to **LISTSERV@UAFSYSB.BITNET** or **LISTSERV@UAFSYSP.UARK.EDU** (use the first address if your university is part of Bitnet; otherwise use the second). Leave the subject line blank (LISTSERV ignores the subject line), and make the following the text of your message:

```
subscribe CAMPCLIM (your name).
```

Usually within 24 hours you will receive a reply in your mailbox that acknowledges your subscription request. You should probably retain a copy of this message. It gives instructions on how to post messages to the list, how to unsubscribe, and how to phrase other commands such as requesting a list of subscribers or accessing the archives. These commands will vary from one group to another if they are using different server programs. Shortly after this message arrives, you will begin receiving mail from the group, which you can read, copy, or save as you would any mail message. A typical subscription acknowledgement message looks like this:

```
Date:            Thu, 5 Jan 1995 10:36:07 -0600
From:            BITNET list server at UAFSYSB (1.8a)
                 <LISTSERV@UAFSYSB.UARK.EDU>
Subject:         You are now subscribed to the CAMPCLIM list
To:              Carol Lea Clark
                 <GR41%UTEP.bitnet@UTEPVM.EP.UTEXAS.EDU>
Reply-To:        CAMPCLIM-Request@UAFSYSB.UARK.EDU
X-LSV-List ID: CAMPCLIM
```

Thu, 5 Jan 1995 10:36:07

Your subscription to the CAMPCLIM list (Campus Climate)
has been accepted.

Please save this message for future reference, especially
if you are not familiar with LISTSERV. This might look
like a waste of disk space now, but in 6 months you will
be glad you saved this information when you realize that
you cannot remember what are the lists you are subscribed
to, or what is the command to leave the list to avoid
filling up your mailbox while you are on vacation. In
fact, you should create a new mail folder for subscription
confirmation messages like this one, and for the "welcome
messages" from the list owners that you will occasionally
receive after subscribing to a new list.

To send a message to all the people currently subscribed
to the list, just send mail to CAMPCLIM@UAFSYSB.UARK.EDU.
This is called "sending mail to the list," because you
send mail to a single address and LISTSERV makes copies
for all the people who have subscribed. This address (CAMP
CLIM@UAFSYSB.UARK.EDU.) is also called the "list address."
You must never try to send any command to that address, as
it would be distributed to all the people who have subscribed. All commands must be sent to the "LISTSERV address," LISTSERV@UAFSYSB.BITNET (or LISTSERV@UAFSYSB.
UARK.EDU). It is very important to understand the difference between the two, but fortunately it is not complicated. The LISTSERV address is like a FAX number, and the
list address is like a normal phone line. If you make your
FAX call someone's regular phone number by mistake, it
will be an unpleasant experience for him but you will
probably be excused the first time. If you do it regularly, however, he will probably get upset and send you a
nasty complaint. It is the same with mailing lists, with
the difference that you are calling hundreds or thousands

of people at the same time, so a lot more people get an-
noyed if you use the wrong number.

You may leave the list at any time by sending a "SIGNOFF
CAMPCLIM" command to LISTSERV@UAFSYSB.BITNET (or LIST-
SERV@UAFSYSB.UARK.EDU). You can also tell LISTSERV how you
want it to confirm the receipt of messages you send to the
list. If you do not trust the system, send a "SET CAMPCLIM
REPRO" command and LISTSERV will send you a copy of your
own messages, so that you can see that the message was
distributed and did not get damaged on the way. After a
while you may find that this is getting annoying, especially if your mail program does not tell you that the
message is from you when it informs you that new mail has
arrived from CAMPCLIM. If you send a "SET CAMPCLIM ACK
NOREPRO" command, LISTSERV will mail you a short acknowledgment instead, which will look different in your mailbox
directory. With most mail programs you will know immediately that this is an acknowledgment you can read later.
Finally, you can turn off acknowledgments completely with
"SET CAMPCLIM NOACK NOREPRO."

Contributions sent to this list are automatically
archived. You can get a list of the available archive
files by sending an "INDEX CAMPCLIM" command to LIST-
SERV@UAFSYSB.BITNET (or LISTSERV@UAFSYSB.UARK.EDU). You
can then order these files with a "GET CAMPCLIM LOGxxxx"
command, or using LISTSERV's database search facilities.
Send an "INFO DATABASE" command for more information on
the latter.

Please note that it is presently possible for other people
to determine that you are signed up to the list through
the use of the "REVIEW" command, which returns the e-mail
address and name of all the subscribers. If you do not
want your name to be visible, just issue a "SET CAMPCLIM
CONCEAL" command.

More information on LISTSERV commands can be found in the
LISTSERV reference card, which you can retrieve by sending
an "INFO REFCARD" command to LISTSERV@UAFSYSB.BITNET (or
LISTSERV@UAFSYSB.UARK.EDU).

Instead of receiving a subscription acknowledgement, you may receive one of the following:

1. An automated error message from your system manager. If this happens, you may have typed the message incorrectly (be sure you type **LISTSERV**, not **LISTSERVE**), or you may have attempted to subscribe to a list that no longer exists or has changed its address.
2. A message from the group list manager asking you to confirm your subscription. Follow the instructions in the request within the time specified.
3. A message stating that you have applied to a group that does not allow open subscription. You may have to supply information to indicate that you meet certain requirements (such as a profession or education level). Follow the instructions in the message.

You use this same LISTSERV address to unsubscribe or to set the message for no mail while you are on vacation. Simply follow the directions in the greeting message you received. Usually you unsubscribe by sending mail to the LISTSERV address with the message, **unsubscribe (name of group)** or **signoff (name of group).** Other commands vary from one mail server program to another. If you need additional commands and are not sure of the exact format, you can send the command "help" to the LISTSERV address.

HOW CAN YOU POST MESSAGES TO THE GROUP?

Each group has a second address which you use to post messages to the group. In order to add your own thoughts to the discussion, you simply write a piece of e-mail and send it to this address (called the list address). This is specified in the greeting message you receive from the group. Remember: *send commands to the LISTSERV address, and send postings to the list address.* This is very important. It can be embarrassing (and ineffective) to send a command such as "unsubscribe" to the list address and have it posted to the whole group. Remember, the LISTSERV address looks like this:

    LISTSERV@(address).

The list address has the list name rather than the word "LISTSERV."

    (name of group)@(address).

A Word About List Etiquette

For most groups it is probably a good idea to read entries for a period of time, perhaps two or three weeks, before you begin posting messages. Doing this is called lurking on a group. Lurking allows you to get a feel for what kinds of messages are appropriate in a particular group. You also will learn what threads, or subjects, the group is discussing. Threads are often initiated by one person posing a question or offering an opinion; then others will offer information and comments. Several of these threads may be going on at the same time and can be identified by the subject lines on the messages. After a while a group will tire of a particular thread or threads and move on to others.

If you post a message that is not consistent with the kind of message typical in a group or if you comment on a thread that is no longer under discussion, you may receive hostile responses from some of the group members. This is called *flaming*.* Many groups are cordial to newcomers if they have taken the time to learn a little about the group before posting. Flaming is frowned upon in many groups, but not all.

FINDING INTERESTING LISTSERVS

There are thousands of LISTSERVs. How do you find ones that interest you? You can start by looking at lists like the one at the end of this chapter. Other Internet books listed in the Appendix may list groups by topic. You can obtain lists and directories of LISTSERV lists at various gopher, World Wide Web, and WAIS sites. An excellent list put together by Diane Kovac is available via electronic mail at **LISTSERV@KENTVM.KENT.EDU** (send the message **GET ACADLIST README F=MAIL**). Also you can join a LISTSERV called NEW–LIST (address **LISTSERV@vm1.nodak.edu**), which is a medium through which individuals and groups announce new groups or query each other about groups on particular topics. Finally, you can obtain lists from LISTSERVs themselves by using the "list global" command.

List Global

If you send the command **list global** to a LISTSERV, you will receive a list of more than 4,000 groups. Simply address the message to any LISTSERV site. You can then download this huge document into your word processor and do a keyword search for the topic that interests you. A better idea, though, might be to reduce the size of the document by sending a more restrictive command. If you add a subject to the command, the LISTSERV will return only addresses of groups that have that word in the list name or description. For example, if you wanted to learn about groups having to do with education, you would issue this command:

```
list global/education.
```

Unfortunately, this method is not completely successful because of the cryptic way group names are sometimes spelled (e.g., an educational group might be listed under **Educ8**).

---

*A flame is a messsage distributed by e-mail, LISTSERV, or USENET intended to insult, provoke, or chastise. Also, as a verb, the act of sending such a message.

WHAT IF YOU MISS PART OF A CONVERSATION?

The content of many groups is automatically archived. You can request a list of archived files, often organized by month, by sending to the LISTSERV address the command **INDEX (name of group).** You can then retrieve a specific file by sending the command **GET (name of group) (filename).**

A group archive can also be searched by keyword. To do this, you use the LISTSERV Command Job Language Interpreter (CJLI), although you don't have to understand all its intricacies. You can take the following template command message and adapt it for your search:

```
//
Database Search DD=Rules
//Rules DD   *
command 1
command 2
/*
```

Address your message to **LISTSERV@(address),** leave the subject line blank, and type the above message, filling in the commands needed to do your search. For example, if you wanted to search CAMPCLIM for entries about basketball, you would type this:

```
//
Database Search DD=Rules
//Rules DD   *
Search basketball in CAMPCLIM
Index
/*
```

If you send this message to the LISTSERV for CAMPCLIM, you will receive an index listing the file numbers and subject lines of postings in which basketball is mentioned. You can then choose which postings look interesting and order them from the LISTSERV with another message. If you wanted postings number 134, 186, 192, and 215, for example, you would send this message:

```
//
Database Search D=Rules
//Rules DD *
Print all of 134, 186, 192, 215
/*
```

A handbook describing LISTSERV database functions in more detail can be obtained by sending the command **INFO DATABASE** to **LISTSERV@BITNIC. bitnet.**

SAMPLE LISTSERV DISCUSSION

The following is part of one thread or conversation on CAMPCLIM. Most groups have several threads going on at the same time, and you can identify them by the subject headings. The names and electronic addresses of the participants have been removed; they would normally appear at the top of each message.

```
Date:        Thu, 27 Oct 1994 15:20:48 -0400
Reply-To:    Campus Climate <CAMPCLIM@UAFSYSB.BITNET>
Sender:      Campus Climate <CAMPCLIM@UAFSYSB.BITNET>
From:        Brian
Subject:     Hazing
```

I wanted to ask some of you about the issue of hazing. I was recently talking with one of my residents, who lives in the complex I supervise. He is a transfer student and is playing football at the JV level. I noticed that he has two black eyes and looks as though he was worked over pretty good by someone. When I asked him what happened, he told me that he was jumped Downtown. He said he did not file a report with anyone and didn't care to because they were just "townies" who jumped him. I found it very strange that this individual was beaten up to this extent, being that he stands about 6'4" and weighs 250 or so. I have also spoken with this individual's roommates and they expressed concern that they were worried about his physical well-being because they know he is pledging a certain football fraternity. This same situation is happening on campus with many male residents. In speaking with other Hall Directors the same thing is occurring to many of their male residents. I realize that our hands are tied until someone reports the hazing, but it isn't going to happen until something tragic occurs. I realize this is an issue across all campuses. What can a person do to shut down some of these fraternity houses that knowingly abuse and beat people. It is very upsetting to see students suffer just to feel part of a group. What can we do????

Brian

```
Sender:      Campus Climate <CAMPCLIM@UAFSYSB.BITNET>
From:        Elizabeth
Subject:     Re: Hazing
In-Reply-To: <199410280110.AA12853@orion.oac.uci.edu>
```

Yes, hazing is a big problem. One of the things that may help is to organize a university-wide task force to confront the issue. Administrations will sometimes begin to take action about hazing if the potential legal liability a university faces is brought to their attention—i.e., colleges can be sued if a fraternity that is officially registered with the university and/or housed on campus injures someone through hazing.

I hate to give you more bad news, but I would suggest that you take a look at Dr. Peggy Sanday's book on "Fraternity Gang-Rape," which documents and researches the role of hazing in encouraging further violence, particularly violence against women.

If anybody on this list is interested, I work with a student-run coalition in the US/Canada that deals with issues of campus sexual violence and related concerns (non-students are involved too). The information and application forms are too lengthy to include here, but I will be happy to forward them to interested parties.

Thanks!
Elizabeth

Date: Fri, 28 Oct 1994 10:00:05 -0400
Reply-To: Campus Climate <CAMPCLIM@UAFSYSB.BITNET>
Sender: Campus Climate <CAMPCLIM@UAFSYSB.BITNET>
From: Monica
Subject: Re: Hazing

Wow! First of all, is hazing illegal in your state? It is
in Massachusetts so that gives us some support. Recently,
this campus, according to newspapers since I cannot break
confidentiality, suspended the captain and another member
of the hockey team for "leading" the hazing/initiation activity of their team. The remaining seniors were placed on
disciplinary probation and barred from playing hockey. The
remainder of the team was placed on probation since all
were at the initiation party and the team by presidential
order had to forfeit the first two games of the season.
Needless to say, this has rocked the campus and has made
the administration the enemy! According to the newspaper,
the students appealed, the two seniors, and they are now
on disc. probation, still barred from hockey, and a few
community service projects. Hazing is illegal and most of
all can lead to unwarranted deaths! If a school does not
take a strong stand, something tragic can happen and the
school will be held responsible. Oh, by the way, the reason the students did not receive suspension was because
the disc. committee, a mix of faculty and students, de-
cided the "hazing" did not occur, that it was just an "un-
safe" party. Interesting.

Sender: Campus Climate <CAMPCLIM@UAFSYSB.BITNET>
From: Necia
Subject: Re: Hazing
In-Reply-To: Message of Thu,
               27 Oct 1994 15:20:48 -0400

Perhaps when they feel good about themselves, and respect
themselves before they come to college—when they feel
strong enough to say no to abuse, just as they need to
feel strong internally to refuse to abuse themselves with
alcohol and other drugs. Also, when people don't equate
the ability to beat up someone else with power and honor
(when the Marines change their slogan to "The few, the
proud, the bullies") perhaps things will improve. Sorry,
no concrete suggestions (beyond packing the offenders in
concrete—ha,ha) TGIF. Necia

```
Date:         Fri, 28 Oct 1994 14:13:00 EDT
Reply-To:     Campus Climate <CAMPCLIM@UAFSYSB.BITNET>
Sender:       Campus Climate <CAMPCLIM@UAFSYSB.BITNET>
From:         Frederic
Subject:      Re: Hazing
```

Brian, Sorry to read about your apparent hazing situation. As a long time dean of students on a campus with 40 plus Greek organizations, I can certainly understand your concern. Hazing is a "phoenix" that never seems to die and encompasses not only Greek organizations but athletic teams, residence halls, and honorary organizations. My advice would be that you contact the Greek advisor or Dean of Students or Vice President for Student Affairs on your campus to share your concerns. All of the national Greek organizations of which I am aware take these issues VERY seriously. I think you'll find a lot of people who would be willing to help. The answer is not to close down these groups, but to find a way - or ways - to eliminate the practice of hazing. Good luck. Fred

```
Date:         Fri, 28 Oct 1994 15:21:10 -0600
Reply-To:
Sender:       Campus Climate <CAMPCLIM@UAFSYSB.BITNET>
From:         Lorene
```

A noted authority on hazing is: Eileen Stevens. Mrs. Stevens's son Chuck was killed in a fraternity hazing incident in the 1970s at Alfred University (NY). She found CHUCK to spread the word about hazing and its consequences. She was instrumental in the passage of New York's anti-hazing law.

Hank Nuwer's book "Broken Pledges: The Deadly Rite of Hazing" (Longstreet Press, 1990. ISBN 092926472X) chronicles Eileen's story and lists hundreds of hazing incidents, court cases, and so forth. Nuwer interviewed a number of sociologists, and their comments on group psychology are enlightening.

Ted Frank's FAQ, found on alt.college.fraternities, is a bibliography of dozens of hazing and fraternity-related books and articles.

Lorene

SELECTED GROUPS

Each group is listed here with two addresses. Use the subscription (sub) address for subscribing to the group and for issuing other LISTSERV commands. Use the list address to post to the list. Note: If your university is not part of Bitnet, you will need to add **.bitnet** to the end of addresses that have a single letter group following the **@** sign. For some university systems this will not work, and you will be limited to non-Bitnet groups.

It is a LISTSERV convention to put addresses in all caps (except for the .bitnet extension) but server programs may recognize either upper or lower case.

ACTNOW-L   (College Activism Information List)
   sub   LISTSERV@BROWNVM.BROWN.EDU
   list   ACTNOW-L@BROWNVM.BROWN.EDU

A "meeting place" where college students can discuss issues relating to college students, faculty, and administration.

CAMPCLIM
   sub   LISTSERV@UAFSYSB.UARK.EDU
   list   CAMPCLIM@UAFSYSB.UARK.EDU

A forum for discussions relating to college campus environments, including student activities, race relations, handicap access, sexual harassment.

CYBERMIND
   sub   MAJORDOMO@WORLD.STU.COM
   list   CYBERMIND@WORLD.STD.COM

A forum for discussion of philosophical and psychological implications of cyberspace.

CURRENT
   sub   CURRENT-REQUEST@TOMAHAWK.WELCH.JHU.EDU
   list   CURRENT@TOMAHAWK.WELCH.JHU.EDU

Discussion, debate, and disagreement about local and world news and politics.

CYBER–L   (Cyber List)
   sub   LISTSERV@MARIST
   list   CYBER-L@MARIST

Discussion group for Bitnet users interested in cyberspace.

DRUGABUS   (Drug Abuse Education Information and Research)
    sub   LISTSERV@UMAB
    list   DRUGABUS@UMAB

Discussions of drug abuse prevention programs and issues.

DSSHE-L   (Disabled Student Services in Higher Education)
    sub   LISTSERV@UBVM
    list   DSSHE-L@UBVM

Purpose is to facilitate the sharing of information regarding students with disabilities and higher education service providers.

EDUCOM-W   (Technology and Education Issues of Interest to Women)
    sub   LISTSERV@BITNIC
    list   EDUCOM-W@BITNIC

Discussion of issues related to women and information technology in higher education.

ENVIRONMENT-L
    sub   LISTSERV@CORNELL.EDU
    list   ENVIRONMENT-L@CORNELL.EDU

Discussion list of topics related to the environment.

FIT-L   (Exercise/Diet/Wellness Talk List)
    sub   LISTSERV@ETSUADMN
    list   FIT–L@ETSUADMN

Discussion of exercise and diet information.

FOODWINE   (Discussion List for Food and Wine)
    sub   LISTSERV@CMUVM.CSV.CMICH.EDU
    list   FOODWINE@CMUVM.CSV.CMICH.EDU

Conversations about food, wine, restaurants, and recipes.

FREETALK   (A list for free talking)
    sub   LISTSERV@BROWNVM
    list   FREETALK@BROWNVM

Members write about any topic.

GRUNGE-L   (Grunge Rock Discussion List)
    sub   LISTSERV@BRUFSC
    list   GRUNGE-L@BRUFSC

Discussion of topics related to grunge rock.

HELP-NET   (Bitnet/Internet Help Resource)
    sub   LISTSERV@TEMPLEVM
    list   HELP-NET@TEMPLEVM

Discussion and solution of questions regarding the Internet and Bitnet.

HIT   (Highly Imaginative Technology and Science Fiction)
    sub   LISTSERV@UFRJ
    list   HIT@UFRJ

Discussions on topics such as cyberpublishing, interactive video, artificial reality, and speech-commanded devices.

H-WOMEN   (H-Net Women's History Discussion List)
    sub   LISTSERV@UICVM
    list   H-WOMEN@UICVM

Discussion of topics related to women's history and rights.

LAWSCH-L   (Law School Discussion List)
    sub   LISTSERV@AUVM
    list   LAWSCH-L@AUVM

Discussion for law school students and those interested in going to law school.

MAC-L   (Macintosh News and Information)
    sub   LISTSERV@YALEVM
    list   MAC-L@YALEVM

Informal discussion of problems and ideas associated with using a Macintosh.

MARKET-L   (MBA School Curriculum Discussion)
    sub   LISTSERV@UCF1VM.CC.UCF.EDU
    LIST   MARKET-L@UCF1VM.CC.UCF.EDU

Issues related to marketing of products and the study of marketing.

MBA-L@MARIST   (MBA School Curriculum Discussion)

```
        sub        LISTSERV@MARISTVM.MARIST.EDU
        list       MBA-L@MARISTVM.MARIST.EDU
```

A forum for administrators, faculty, and MBA students to discuss MBA programs, their administration, and issues.

```
MEDSTU-L          (Medical Student Discussion List)
        sub        LISTSERV@UNMVMA
        list       MEDSTU-L@UNMVMA
```

A discussion group for medical school students and those interested in attending medical school.

```
NEW-LIST
        sub        LISTSERV@VM1.NODAK.EDU
        list       NEW-LIST@VM1.NODAK.EDU
```

Announcements posted of new LISTSERV groups.

```
RECYCLE           (Recycling in Practice)
        sub        LISTSERV@UNMVMA
        list       RECYCLE@UMAB
```

Discussion of recycling programs and related issues.

```
VIRCOLL           (Virtual College of Neighborhood Study)
        sub        LISTSERV@SJUVM.STJOHNS.EDU
        list       VIRCOLL@SJUVM.STJOHNS.EDU
```

Uses the form of a college to address specific problems of residential and other communities such as workplaces.

```
VIRTED            (Virtual Reality and Education)
        sub        LISTSERV@SJUVM.STJOHNS.EDU
        list       VIRTED@SJUVM.STJOHNS.EDU
```

Discussion of the uses of virtual reality in education.

```
WIN3-L            (Microsoft Windows Forum)
        sub        LISTSERV@UICVM.UIC.EDU
        list       WIN3-L@UICVM.UIC.EDU
```

Discussion of Windows issues and problems at all levels of expertise.

ASSIGNMENTS

1. Subscribe to three LISTSERVs and lurk for two weeks, reading the entries posted. Write a memo comparing the three groups.
2. After lurking on several groups for two or three weeks, write a sample posting which contributes to one of the threads of a group. As directed by your instructor, submit it for review, and post it to the group.
3. Using some of the methods suggested in the chapter, find three other LISTSERV groups that interest you. Subscribe to them, lurk for a period of time, and write a review of each group to circulate in your class.
4. After lurking on several groups, discuss the experience with a small group. Working together, compile a group report about the experience of participating in LISTSERVs.
5. Do a subject search with a LISTSERV of your choice. Obtain the entries suggested by the subject search.
6. Obtain the Bitnet handbook detailing LISTSERV functions mentioned on page 37. Write a memo about additional commands not mentioned in this chapter which might be useful for searching a LISTSERV database.

QUESTIONS TO ASK

1. Is your university system part of Bitnet? If not, how does your university recommend sending mail between Bitnet and you?
2. Do you have an on-line list of LISTSERVs on your university's system?
3. What policies does your university have regarding LISTSERVs (because of high volume of mail, some universities restrict subscriptions)?

F I V E

USENET
NEWSGROUPS

U SENET IS AN INCREDIBLY LARGE COLLECTION of electronic discussion groups called newsgroups. It may also be the largest decentralized information entity in existence. Currently, there are more than 8,000 USENET newsgroups, and that number is growing every day. The newsgroups provide forums for people all over the world to discuss anything and everything; some groups are serious, others are humorous, others controversial. Topics range from architecture to zoology, from particle physics to woodcarving. Some of the groups are so intriguing that enthusiasts spend a good part of their time just reading and interacting on USENET. For some people, USENET *is* the Internet because it is the only network service that they use.

Created in 1979, USENET, predates many of the current Internet protocols. It was originally implemented as a separate UUCP (Unix to Unix Copy) based network. This means that while all Internet sites can carry USENET, so can many non-Internet sites. As USENET has been integrated into the Internet, it has become an invaluable resource to users of all ages and vocations.

This is the magic of USENET: Anyone, anywhere in the world, can say whatever they want about any subject, in front of an audience of thousands, sometimes millions, and anyone in that audience can respond. USENET is a great equalizer. People are judged by their ideas, thoughts, and ability to communicate rather than by their age, weight, sex, or skin color. Through USENET you can discuss your favorite hobby, state political opinions, or ask technical questions, and you can expect replies from all over the world.

The process for accessing USENET is quite different from that for subscribing to LISTSERVs. You don't subscribe to USENET through your electronic mail facility, and the postings to the group don't come into your mailbox in a regular fashion as they do with LISTSERVs. In a sense, you go to USENET groups, rather than having them come to you. You access groups with a software program called a news reader, such as nn or rn (Unix), nnr or netnews (IBM CMS), or VMS-News (Vax VMS). Anyone can post a message; the postings are distributed worldwide and can be read by anyone who is able to access USENET.

Not all university systems offer a connection to USENET, and those that do usually offer only portions of the 8,000 or so groups. You will need to find out from your instructor, university help desk, or system administrator whether your system supports USENET. If it does not, you still have the option of reading group messages through a gopher server, by e-mail, or via the World Wide Web (see the discussion later in this chapter).

WHAT CAN YOU EXPECT FROM USENET?

USENET, despite its enormous size, or perhaps because of it, has a very limited organizational structure. Any person or organization with a computer on which to store the messages and with a connection to the network can become part of USENET.

USENET groups are either moderated or unmoderated. In a moderated group an individual or small group receives all the messages and screens them before they are posted to the group. The moderator eliminates postings that are considered irrelevant or objectionable.

Unmoderated groups, on the other hand, are open for anyone to post anything. The messages of unmoderated groups are controlled by peer pressure, because any posting can be followed by postings that criticize or contradict it. Thus USENET groups are self-policing, enforcing standards of netiquette (Internet etiquette) and discouraging commercial use. Some users find this lack of centralized authority liberating, while others find it exasperating. Discussions are often heated, and, especially in some groups, individuals freely flame each other. Still, USENET groups offer an incredible richness of experience that makes them especially helpful to students who are looking for information about an issue or research problem.

HOW DO YOU KNOW WHAT GROUPS ARE OF INTEREST?

USENET is loosely organized by subject. Groups are broken down into broad categories, indicated by a prefix identifier. The most commonly distributed ones are the following:

alt	Alternative groups covering a wide variety of topics
biz	Business

clari	ClariNet—live from UPI wire service
comp	Computers, computer science, and software-related discussions
K-12	Teachers and students K–12
misc	Other
news	News about USENET
rec	Hobbies and recreation
sci	Scientific, research-oriented topics
soc	Social issues, world cultures
talk	Debate and lengthy discussions

Many systems also carry subject areas that deal with a specific region or language. For example, the **utexas** hierarchy contains information pertaining to the University of Texas, and the **fj** hierarchy contains Japanese language postings.

The prefix identifier is followed by a more specific name of the major subject area. For example, a group with the name **comp.graphics.animation** focuses on the technical aspects of computer animation.

SUGGESTED GROUPS FOR NEW USERS

New users should check out the standard articles in the newsgroups **news.announce.newusers** and **news.answers.** There you will find a FAQ (Frequently Asked Questions) document about USENET, a list of active newsgroups, and other useful documents. Another helpful group is **news.questions,** a place where newcomers can post questions and more experienced USENET users will answer them. It is a good idea to read some of the articles in the **news.announce.newusers** and **news.answers** groups to try to answer basic questions for yourself before posting questions to **news.questions.**

THE "ALT.BINARIES" HIERARCHIES

If your news server carries the **alt** category of newsgroups, you may have access to several newsgroups that begin with the title **alt.binaries.** Binary is the format used by FTP sites to store software, digital images, sounds, and just about anything else that is not text. These newsgroups contain those same kinds of items, posted by members of the USENET community. Special commands, translators, and software compression utilities may be necessary for you to make use of the postings found in these groups. However, if you have the capability and know-how to use these groups, you can access a wealth of pictures, sounds, and occasionally software, and also gain a forum through which you can distribute your own artistic creations and favorite shareware to thousands of other users.

HOW ARE MESSAGES STORED AND TRANSMITTED?

Your university system, if it supports USENET, stores a copy of all recent USENET messages, which any number of people can read upon demand. The system communicates regularly with other USENET nodes and both accepts and transmits new messages. Periodically old messages are removed from groups as new ones arrive. Some of the newsgroups create archives of the old messages which can be accessed in a number of ways, depending on the group. (A group's FAQ usually notes the location of the archive and how to access it.)

HOW DO YOU READ USENET NEWSGROUPS?

As with many of the protocols on the Internet, there are a number of pieces of software through which you can access USENET news. Which news reader you use will depend upon the type and speed of your connection as well as the type of computer and operating system; beyond that, your decision will depend upon your own personal preference. The following example was created with the Net News reader on a VAX workstation running the VMS operating system. While it may differ slightly from the reader you are using, the concepts are the same.

The first thing you need to do is load your news reader. In this case, you would type **news** at the command prompt. On a UNIX system the most common news readers are rn and nn, both of which you can load by typing their name at the command prompt. IBM-VM systems also make use of the rn reader. A network, SLIP, or PPP connected PC may use Trumpet, and a Mac might use Nuntius or NewsWatcher, each of which can be loaded by a click of the mouse. See the section "Popular News-Reading Software" at the end of this chapter for more information about each of these readers.

When you load a news reader, it looks at the list of newsgroups available to you. On UNIX and VMS machines, this list is usually stored in a file named **.newsrc.** On other machines it may be under a different name, but there is usually an equivalent file. When you subscribe to a group, or unsubscribe, or make other basic changes with your news reader, the changes are made in the **.newsrc** file. As it loads, the news reader looks at this file to find out which newsgroups you subscribe to, then retrieves information about those groups.

Once the news reader is finished retrieving the newsgroups to which you have subscribed, you may need to decide whether to join any new groups. If a new group has been added to those available at your site, your news reader will ask you whether you wish to subscribe. New groups spring up all the time, and several groups may appear on one day. If there are no new groups, you can move on to the next step right away. In some cases the first time you use your news reader may prove to be a time-consuming session, because you may start with an empty **.newsrc** file and so your news reader will consider every group a new group and will ask you whether you wish to join each one. If your site has access to upwards of 4,000 groups, this process can take a very long time. Be patient. You should have to go through that process only once.

In most cases the first time you load your news reader, you will automatically be subscribed to all of the newsgroups available at your site. After the reader has loaded, you will be given a list like the following:

```
NEWSGROUPS  [ALL, 4793 Newsgroups]

              Newsgroup                          Count      Unread
->  1    _ alt.0d                                  334        334
    2    _ alt.2600                              12352      12352
    3    _ alt.2600.hope.announce                   15         15
    4    _ alt.2600.hope.d                           3          3
    5    _ alt.2600.hope.tech                       22         22
    6    _ alt.2600hz                               25         25
    7    _ alt.3d                                  249        249
    8    _ alt.3d.studio                            75         75
    9    _ alt.aapg.announce                         0          0
   10    _ alt.aapg.general                          1          1
   11    _ alt.abortion                             17         17
   12    _ alt.abortion.inequity                   630        630
   13    _ alt.abuse-recovery                        0          0
   14    _ alt.abuse.recovery                      165        165
   15    _ alt.abuse.transcendence                 124        124
   16    _ alt.acme.exploding.newsgroup            111        111
   17    _ alt.activism                          10171      10171
   18    _ alt.activism.d                          632        632
NEWS>
```

This is the beginning of the list of nearly 5,000 newsgroups available through this connection. At the right-hand side of the screen are the number of postings currently in each group, followed by the number of postings that you have not yet read. This information can be useful for keeping track of which groups you read most often. At the bottom of the screen is the prompt (NEWS>) for this news reader, and in front of the numeral 1 on **alt.0d** is a pointer indicating which group is currently selected.

At this point you could begin to unsubscribe to some groups, leaving just those in which you are interested (ask your instructor or system administrator how to subscribe and unsubscribe using your reader). However, rather than doing that, it might be beneficial to have a look around. Scrolling through the newsgroup list, you may note many topics that interest you. For example, if you are a looking for that perfect recipe with which to impress a friend or significant other, the group **rec.food.recipes** might be just what you have been searching for.

```
NEWSGROUPS [ALL, 4793 Newsgroups]

                  Newsgroup                            Count    Unread
     4041  _ rec.crafts.textiles.yarn                    164      164
     4042  _ rec.crafts.winemaking                       184      184
     4043  _ rec.equestrian                             6028     6028
     4044  _ rec.folk-dancing                            176      176
     4045  _ rec.food.cooking  .                        4838     4838
     4046  _ rec.food.drink                              874      874
     4047  _ rec.food.drink.beer                         247      247
     4048  _ rec.food.drink.coffee                       190      190
     4049  _ rec.food.historic                            78       78
     4050  _ rec.food.preserving                          17       17
-->  4051  _ rec.food.recipes        .                   246       69
     4052  _ rec.food.restaurants                        191      191
     4053  _ rec.food.sourdough                           71       71
     4054  _ rec.food.veg                                474      474
     4055  _ rec.food.veg.cooking                        225      225
     4056  _ rec.gambling                               1964     1964
     4057  _ rec.games.abstract                           29       29
     4058  _ rec.games.backgammon                        112      112
NEWS>  █
```

Upon entering that group, you will find a listing like the following:

```
rec.food.recipes: 72 Items (#11191 - #11436) Reg:1  Srv:newshost.cc.utexas.edu
        -<Recipes for interesting food and drink. (Moderated)>-
        Title                              From             Lines   Date
-->11191  rec.food.cooking Commonly Discussed To arielle@taronga.com  1175  25-Feb
   11366  Family BBQ Sauce Recipe             TURNER7@applelink.a    33  14-Mar
   11367  Bread Pudding                       Martha Muzychka <mu    25  14-Mar
   11368  Nestle Zebra Striped Cookie Bars    chanhan@uclink.berk    25  14-Mar
   11369  REQUESTS from Mon Mar 13, 1995      phill@rt66.com (Pat    45  14-Mar
   11370  Pasta salad (good for picnics)      NORVELLE@uga.cc.uga    19  14-Mar
   11371  Vietnamese Recipes                  pcharles@iastate.ed   712  12-Mar
   11372  Collection: About 20 Indian Recipes (3 pcharles@iastate.ed 1026  12-Mar
   11373  Homemade Yogurt                     NORVELLE@uga.cc.uga    27  14-Mar
   11374  Chinese Chicken Salad Dressing      easg173@taurus.oac.    18  14-Mar
   11375  Hunan Blend                         hunt@austin.metrowe    45  14-Mar
   11376  Fresh Tomato-Basil Sauce            CBrunelli@aol.com (    23  14-Mar
   11377  Corn Spoon Bread (like Chi Chi's)   skthom@ccmail.monsa    44  13-Mar
   11378  Easter-Egg Bread                    bmcswain@email.unc.    40  14-Mar
   11379  Bagel Instructions (long)           hunt@austin.metrowe   177  15-Mar
   11380  Crusty Puffed Potatoes              "C.C." <ccw8u@poe.a    26  15-Mar
   11381  REQUESTS from Wed Mar 15, 1995      phill@rt66.com (Pat   204  16-Mar
   11382  Cranberry Pork Roast                rorsini@iadfw.net (    36  16-Mar
NEWS>
```

This is the beginning of the list of postings in this newsgroup. At the top of
the screen is the name of the group, under which is the topic line for that group:
"Recipes for interesting food and drink." This line also tells you that the group is
moderated. The list is numbered just like the list of newsgroups, and each posting

is listed with the subject, the e-mail address of the person who posted it, the length of the posting in lines, and the date on which it was posted.

Now what should you have for dessert? Cookie Bars? Nestle Zebra Striped Cookie Bars? Why not? Moving the cursor down to number 11368, you can select the article about this sweet treat, as shown below.

```
rec.food.recipes: 72 Items (#11191 - #11436) Reg:1  Srv:newshost.cc.utexas.edu
        -<Recipes for interesting food and drink. (Moderated)>-
            Title                                From          Lines Date
  11191   rec.food.cooking Commonly Discussed To arielle@taronga.com  1175 25-Feb
  11366   Family BBQ Sauce Recipe                TURNER7@applelink.a   33 14-Mar
  11367   Bread Pudding                          Martha Muzychka <mu   25 14-Mar
->11368   Nestle Zebra Striped Cookie Bars       chanhan@uclink.berk   25 14-Mar
  11369   REQUESTS from Mon Mar 13, 1995         phill@rt66.com (Pat   45 14-Mar
  11370   Pasta salad (good for picnics)         NORVELLE@uga.cc.uga   19 14-Mar
  11371   Vietnamese Recipes                     pcharles@iastate.ed  712 12-Mar
  11372   Collection: About 20 Indian Recipes (3 pcharles@iastate.ed 1026 12-Mar
  11373   Homemade Yogurt                        NORVELLE@uga.cc.uga   27 14-Mar
  11374   Chinese Chicken Salad Dressing         easg173@taurus.oac.   18 14-Mar
  11375   Hunan Blend                            hunt@austin.metrowe   45 14-Mar
  11376   Fresh Tomato-Basil Sauce               CBrunelli@aol.com (  23 14-Mar
  11377   Corn Spoon Bread (like Chi Chi's)      skthom@ccmail.monsa   44 13-Mar
  11378   Easter-Egg Bread                       bmcswain@email.unc.   40 13-Mar
  11379   Bagel Instructions (long)              hunt@austin.metrowe  177 15-Mar
  11380   Crusty Puffed Potatoes                 "C.C." <ccw8u@poe.a   26 15-Mar
  11381   REQUESTS from Wed Mar 15, 1995         phill@rt66.com (Pat  204 16-Mar
  11382   Cranberry Pork Roast                   rorsini@iadfw.net (   36 16-Mar
NEWS>
```

Select the article and *presto*, there's the recipe!

```
Group: rec.food.recipes, Item 11368   (Range: #11191 - #11436, Unread: 69)
Subject: Nestle Zebra Striped Cookie Bars
From: chanhan@uclink.berkeley.edu (Shu-Han Chen), University of California, Berk
Date: 14 Mar 95 07:20:09 CST

Got this from the Sunday Coupons..

Nestle Zebra Stripe Cookie Bars (Makes 20 bars)

1 package (18oz) Nestle Refrigerated Chocolate Chip Cookie Dough
1/2 package Nestle Refrigerated Chocolate Chocolate Chip Cookie Dough

Press whole package of chocolate chip dough onto greased baking sheet
into 13" x 9" rectangle.

Divide 1/2 package of chocolate chocolate chip cookie dough into 12 portions.
With hands, roll each portion into a 9" long strip; place strips 1/2" apart
across the width of the rectangle.

Bake in center of preheated 350 degree oven, 14-18 minutes, or until edge
is set, and center is still slightly soft.  Cool; cut into bars.
NEWS>
<RETURN for more - 16/25 Lines (79%)>
```

After having explored this group, you know that the group posts recipes rather than having discussions about cookbook sales statistics. In some groups the distinction is not clear. It may be useful to lurk, just reading postings for a couple of days before adding your two cents to the discussion.

Threads

When some of the more advanced readers are used, the contents of each group can be loosely organized into threads. A thread is a topic being discussed in a newsgroup. For example, the group **rec.travel.rv** may contain ongoing discussions about the best recreational vehicles on the market, a particular RV park outside of Yellowstone National Park, and tips for avoiding repair scams. Messages relating to a particular discussion are threaded together so that they can all be read at once. For example, the thread about the RV park near Yellowstone might contain an initial posting from a person who had stayed there and enjoyed it enough to recommend it to other newsgroup members. This might be followed by a posting asking for specific directions to the park, one asking what prices to expect, and one answering both of these questions. There might be a posting from a dissatisfied traveler who disagrees with the original posting. Many news readers allow you to issue a command to present messages organized by threads, enabling you to read items on a particular topic consecutively.

Posting

A posting, or post, is any message sent to a newsgroup. Postings differ from e-mail because they are broadcast rather than transmitted point to point. Anyone can post a message to a newsgroup. Most news readers are equipped with a text editor which allows you to create postings. Later these postings are transmitted to your news server and from there to every other USENET news server in the world. All you have to do is write it and post it. When you post a message to a newsgroup, you have the option of continuing an ongoing thread or creating a new one. Finally, remember that when you post a message you are submitting it to the public—to hundreds of nations and thousands, perhaps millions, of people, so be sure to take appropriate caution with what you say. If you are nervous about making your first post and wish to try a test run first, you can post to the group **misc.test.**

A WORD ABOUT USENETIQUETTE

No matter what part of the Internet you are using, it is important to observe basic rules of netiquette, or etiquette of the Internet. Doing this is doubly important when posting to USENET, because your contribution, and your breaches of netiquette, are laid out before an audience of millions.

The first rule of Usenetiquette is lurk before you post. Spend some time observing and trying to get the gist of the conversation before jumping in with your own opinion. While it won't help pay for property damage if your house burns down, lurking can certainly prevent flames. A flame is a posting or e-mail message intended to insult, rebuke, or provoke. To break netiquette is to invite flames, and on USENET this can mean flames from around the world. Remember that when you post to USENET, your e-mail address goes with your posting, and people won't hesitate to send flames directly to your mailbox. In fact, flames have become such an important part of USENET that there are groups devoted entirely to flaming.

The following are some other important netiquette guidelines:

1. If you disapprove of the topic of a discussion group, leave the group alone. Disruptive postings and off-subject postings are not appreciated and will most likely result in a mailbox full of flames.
2. Read the FAQ list. Most groups will periodically post a frequently asked questions list which details the most common topics of conversation in a group and answers many of the basic questions relating to those topics. If you post a simple question to the group, someone may politely inquire whether or not you have read the FAQ. On the other hand, you may get flamed by someone irritated at seeing the question for the $6.2*10^{22}$ time.
3. Don't shout. In USENET, words in CAPITAL LETTERS are considered shouting. While it may occasionally be appropriate to shout, don't post entire messages in uppercase.
4. Finally, remember to do unto others as you would have them do unto you. This is a long-standing rule on USENET. Once you get the hang of things, sending flaming messages can be a lot of fun. Remember, however, that there is a real person who receives your flame. Don't send messages you wouldn't want to receive.

USENET VIA GOPHER AND WWW

If your site does not support USENET directly, you can still read newsgroups through gopher servers and the World Wide Web. A few gopher sites offer limited numbers of USENET groups which can be read through their gopher servers (see Chapter 8 for information on how gopher works). One of these sites is at Virginia Polytechnic Institute and State University. You can reach this gopher directly by typing, at your gopher prompt, **gopher.vt.edu.** At the root menu of this gopher, select option "News, Schedules and Events," then "USENET NewsServers/" and you will receive another menu which contains a number of USENET news servers. Most of these sites restrict access because of the large amount of traffic, but at publication time several were still unrestricted. Try Walla Walla College, **news.wwc.edu;** University of Canberra, **services.canberra.edu.au;** or Birmingham University, **san4.bham.ac.uk.**

USENET access is also possible via the World Wide Web (see Chapter 7). Some World Wide Web sites, such as **http://www.apple.com,** may offer a limited number of groups pertaining to a certain subject (this Apple site carries several **comp.mac** groups which discuss Macintosh related issues). With some advanced graphical Web browsers, it is even possible to access your own news host (ask your instructor or system administrator for the address) and both read and post to groups without ever leaving your Web browser.

POPULAR NEWS-READING SOFTWARE

Read News (rn) is one of the most commonly available news readers for time-sharing environments, with versions available for UNIX, CMS, VMS, and several other popular platforms. Unfortunately, this versatility comes with a price: The rn news reader is one of the older ones and can be difficult to use. When using the rn reader, the more groups you are subscribed to, the more difficult the reader becomes to manage. Also the one- or two-letter commands used by rn can appear cryptic. A newer and simpler version of rn called trn (Threaded Read News) is used at some sites, solving a lot of the quirks of the old reader.

No News (nn) is a little newer than rn and is available chiefly on UNIX platforms. No News is better suited than Read News to the large number of newsgroups and postings that USENET currently supports. In order to allow you to browse through the groups easily, the nn reader shows you a list of all the articles in the groups you subscribe to, similar to the list in the example in this chapter, and easily allows you to select those articles you wish to read while skipping over those you do not. The nn reader also groups together messages with the same heading so that you can see the connections between articles.

One of the newest news readers available for UNIX is the tin reader. This reader uses threading to organize the articles within each group, to make chains of conversation easier to follow. This reader also offers a menu-based interface and fairly simple command structure.

If you are using a PC or Macintosh connected directly to the Internet (in a networked lab or at home via a PPP or SLIP connection), you may have a number of options when choosing a news reader. The most common news reader for the PC is Trumpet, which contains a lot of nice features and is relatively simple to use. The two most common Macintosh news readers are Nuntius, a reader that organizes the newsgroups into folders, which can be opened just like any folder on the Macintosh; and NewsWatcher, which organizes posts by threads and includes an easy-to-use editor for creating postings and composing e-mail.

USENET GROUPS OF INTEREST

news.announce.newusers	Articles about USENET
news.newusers.questions	Questions asked about USENET
news.announce.new groups	Announcements about new groups
news.answers	FAQs from different newsgroups
alt.Internet.services	Questions asked about Internet

| alt.infosystems.announce | Announcements of new information services on the Internet |
| misc.text | Group where new users can practice posting before posting to another group |

ASSIGNMENTS

1. Determine how to access USENET at your university. Access a news reader and read the standard postings in **news.announce.newusers** and **news. newusers.questions.** Discuss in your small group what you learned.
2. Explore groups in one category such as **comp** or **biz.** Make a list of groups that seem of interest and read recent postings. Share this information with your group or class.
3. Locate five groups that relate to your major or other area of interest. Read the postings in these groups, and write a memo about what you find.
4. Choose a group that relates to your major or topic area, and lurk in the group for a week or more. Write an audience analysis of the group, including characteristics of the individuals you can determine from reading their postings, topics under discussion, general tone of the postings, and degree of acceptance of newcomers. Then prepare a message for the group and, after having it reviewed by a fellow student, send it to the group for posting.
5. Write a memo comparing the experience of reading USENET and LISTSERV groups. Include an analysis of ease of access as well as relevance of the groups to your area of interest.
6. Write a guide to USENET for people in your major. Include instructions on how to use a news reader, information on how to select groups of interest, and a list of relevant groups.

QUESTIONS TO ASK

1. Does your university system have USENET access?
2. What USENET news readers are available to you? How do you access them?
3. Is there a handout or on-line manual that lists the commands for your news reader?
4. How do you subscribe and unsubscribe to a particular newsgroup?
5. How do you read postings?
6. How do you send a posting?
7. How do you save a posting?
8. How do you exit from the news reader?

SIX

REAL-TIME COMMUNICATION: TALK, CHAT, IRC, AND MUDS

E LECTRONIC MAIL, LISTSERVs, and USENET newsgroups enable the individual user to cross spatial boundaries and communicate easily with people around the globe. Real-time communication tools such as TALK, MUDs, and IRC take the process a step further because they make it possible to communicate interactively with other users rather than simply responding to each other's messages. Person-to-person utilities such as TALK and CHAT allow users to send messages back and forth interactively, as in an on-screen telephone conversation or conference call. IRC (Internet Relay Chat) uses a system of channels whereby hundreds of users can hold real-time discussions on a wide range of topics. Finally, MUDs offer real-time communication within a fictional setting.

SIMPLE REAL-TIME COMMUNICATION: TALK

The most basic forms of real-time communication on the Internet are the person-to-person utilities. These programs allow you to contact another user directly, much the same way that e-mail does, but in real time. The simplest way to access this type of utility may be via the command prompt on your time-sharing system, although some versions of these programs have been developed for SLIP, PPP, and network-connected computers as well as for menu-driven systems. The most widely used and universally available person-to-person utility is TALK.

TALK is a visual communication program which copies lines typed on your screen to that of another user, and copies lines typed there back to your own screen. If you wish to TALK to someone on your own system (the same host and domain that you are logged in to), then at the command prompt you type

```
talk name
```

where **name** is the user name of the person you are trying to reach. If the person is on a different system (different host or domain), then you would type

```
talk name@hostname.domainname
```

where **name** is the user name of the person you are trying to reach, and **hostname** and **domainname** make up the address of the system the person is on.

When you have done this, TALK will contact the person you wish to talk to. First TALK checks to see whether or not that person is logged in and receiving messages. If not, it indicates so with an error message. Otherwise TALK will send a message to the person to whom you wish to talk (for this example, you are assumed to be **Smith@candy.usw.edu** trying to contact **Frodo@warsaw.uswe.edu**). The message will include information similar to this:

```
talk: connection requested by Smith@candy.usw.edu
talk: respond with: talk Smith@candy.usw.edu
```

At this point Frodo, the recipient of the message, should reply by typing

```
talk Smith@candy.usw.edu
```

This will establish a link between you and the person to whom you want to talk. At this point your screen display will divide in two horizontally, the top half displaying what you type and the bottom half displaying what the other person types, allowing you both to type simultaneously. Typing **^L** (**Ctrl-L**) will cause the screen to be reformatted in case it begins to look messy. To exit from TALK, just type an interrupt character; on most systems this is **^C** (**Ctrl-C**). TALK will move the cursor to the bottom of the screen and return you to the command prompt.

If someone contacts you with TALK, you are not obligated to reply, any more than you are obligated to answer the phone. If you ignore the message requesting a TALK session, after a few minutes TALK will issue a message to the other party stating that you are not responding. If you don't wish to be bothered by any single talk requests, you can turn away all incoming requests by using the **mesg** command. To disable incoming requests, type **mesg n** at the command prompt. To begin receiving requests again, type **mesg y** at the command prompt.

MULTI-USER REAL-TIME COMMUNICATION: CHAT

The next level of real-time Internet communication is simple multi-user communication. Multi-user communication programs allow several users to communicate with each other in a conference-like setting, through the use of public and private messages in a forum. Most programs of this nature allow for communication only between people on the same network or computer system; however, some have been modified to allow access from users across the Internet. Like person-to-person real-time communication programs, multi-user programs are accessed most simply at the command prompt of your time-sharing system, although versions for network, SLIP, PPP, and menu-based systems do exist. One popular multi-user communication utility is CHAT.

CHAT is based on an idea that evolved among the bulletin board system community of the early 1980s. Bulletin board systems, or BBSs, are local multi-user networks, often consisting of no more than a personal computer configured to support two or three modem lines. These systems provide a "bulletin board" where users can post public messages similar to USENET news and utilities for sending e-mail to other users on the same system. Over the years numerous large BBSs developed, with multiple modem lines to accommodate a greater number of users. Once multiple lines were in place, allowing several participants to use the system simultaneously, a demand for real-time communication arose. The tradition of both public (bulletin board postings) and private (e-mail) communication continued through the development of CHAT and similar programs.

If you have access to CHAT, you simply need to type

```
chat forumname
```

at the command prompt, where **forumname** is the name of the forum you wish to enter. Each forum discusses a different topic, much the way that the USENET newsgroups do, and many forums may exist on a single computer system. CHAT will connect you to the conversation going on in the forum you choose. Your display screen will be divided into two parts, a large space which contains the discussion, and a line on which you type your messages. Unlike TALK, CHAT does not relay each character as it is typed. Rather, to say something, simply type what you want to say, one line at a time, and press <ENTER> between each line. When you press <ENTER>, the line is transmitted to the rest of the users in the forum. In order to tell who is saying what, CHAT automatically adds each user's name to the beginning of each line he or she types.

CHAT also allows private messages between individuals. While commands do vary from system to system, the most common private message command is **/msg.** In order to send a private message to another user, you would type

```
/msg username
```

followed by the message that you wish to send, where **username** is the name of the user who is to receive the message. When you press <ENTER>, the message will be sent only to the screen of the user you specify; this is akin to whispering in somebody's ear at a meeting. No one else, with the possible exception of the sys-op, will be able to see the message you sent.

The sys-op is the user who owns or administrates the system. The sys-op can use a reserved set of powerful, systemwide commands which allow him or her to view any message, public or private, and to address all users simultaneously. The sys-op can even remove or bar a user from a forum.

Most CHAT systems have a basic command structure allowing the use of several interesting options, including password-protected entry to some forums, and semi-public messages, akin to whispering to a small group of people all at once. However, if you do not have access to a system that supports CHAT, or if you feel limited by the number of people or forums in it, then you may want to try something a little different: IRC.

WHAT IS IRC?

IRC (Internet Relay Chat) is a synchronous, multi-user, text-based communications system. That is, IRC allows true text conversations among many people around the world simultaneously. It has been called Internet CB radio. That's not a bad analogy, because it even uses channels in a similar fashion. However IRC, with host systems in more than twenty countries, is truly international; when you log on to a channel, you may be talking with students in Singapore or Israel as well as at your own university. On IRC you can join an existing channel or create a private one for yourself and a friend or two.

The difference between IRC and other synchronous text-based systems is purely one of scale. While TALK is a person-to-person communication tool, and CHAT allows a few users to communicate simultaneously in a public conference style, IRC allows thousands of people to converse simultaneously through both public and person-to-person messages.

The fundamental building blocks of IRC are channels. At any given moment there may be as many as 3,000 channels, each with an active conversation between a number of users. When you first enter IRC, you are not able to see the activity of or interact with other users. In order to begin, you need to join a channel. You first specify the name of a channel. If a channel with that name exists, you will be added to the list of people on that channel, and you will be able to converse with them. If no channel by that name exists, the IRC program will create a new channel under that name and will place you in charge of it. This new channel may then be joined by other users.

IRC can support an effectively unlimited number of channels. A channel can have any name, but the name generally indicates the nature of the conversation it carries. For example, "Chicago" is a meeting place for users from Chicago, and users in "darkbar" mimic the conversation in a bar or lounge.

In many ways, IRC is like a vastly expanded version of CHAT. The main difference is that IRC is an Internet-wide protocol supported by many large servers around the world. Just as CHAT manages forums, IRC keeps track of who has joined which channels and ensures that only people within the same channel can see each other's typed messages. However, unlike CHAT forums, IRC channels are not limited to users connected to a specific computer system or network. Anyone, anywhere on the Internet can connect to IRC and create or join a channel.

The user who initially creates a channel is known as a channel operator, or chanop, and has certain privileges. For example, the chanop may change the mode of the channel, that is, may instruct IRC to limit the number of users allowed within a channel, may limit entry to those people specifically invited to join the channel, may guard entry to the channel with a password, may kick another user off the channel, or may even confer chanop privileges on one or more other users. For more information on using these commands, refer to the IRC on-line help system by typing **/help** at the IRC command line.

There is a set of IRC commands that are even more powerful than those available to a chanop. The ability to address all IRC users at once and to remove a user from IRC altogether is reserved for the people who run and maintain the IRC network connections. These superusers or opers have access to the actual computer programs that make up IRC and thus have virtually unlimited ability to manipulate the IRC environment.

HOW DO YOU ACCESS IRC?

Your university system may or may not support IRC. To find out, try typing **IRC** at the command prompt. If this does not work, ask around, or if you have a menu-driven system, look for IRC as a menu item. A few IRC programs, such as Homer and IRCle, have been developed for network, SLIP, and PPP connected personal computers. If you have trouble determining whether you have access, ask your system administrator for advice.

When you first connect to IRC, you will enter the null channel. As with CHAT, there will be a space across the bottom of your screen where you type your messages, and you transmit the messages one line at a time by pressing <ENTER>. Each message is prefaced with the nick, or nickname, of the person who sent it.

To display a short introduction to IRC, type **/help intro.** In order to join a channel, you would type **/join #channel,** where channel is the name of the channel you wish to join. For a list of the names of all the channels and the topics they are discussing, type **/list.** This is a rather long list, so users with a slow connection may wish to avoid using this command too frequently. If you want to create a channel, simply pick a name not currently being used and type **/join #channel.**

If you connect to a busy channel, the text may seem confusing at first, and the messages may come in so fast that you may feel you can't read them all. Also, users who frequent certain channels develop a set of words with private meanings that newbies (or new users) may not understand. If you do not find a particular channel congenial, try another.

SOME BASIC IRC COMMANDS:

/help	Displays help screen
/list	Lists all available public channels, topics, and number of users currently logged on
/m name	Sends private message to person with that name
/nick	Designates or changes your nickname

/query name	Begins a private conversation with the named person (That person needs to type the same command for conversation to be completely private.) End by typing **/query.**
/quit	Quits IRC
/signoff	Quits IRC
/topic	Announces topic for channel you create. For example, **/topic chocolate** indicates chocolate is the topic of that channel.
/who <chan>	Displays e-mail addresses of those on a particular channel
/whois name	Shows information about a user who is on-line
/whois *	Shows information about all users on-line

A conversation on IRC might look like this:

```
<smug> hyk: i know
<smug> :D
<smug> mimi: i am grrreat! how R you??
* Hyker lowers the disco ball
* Mimi just got new glasses today :( *ACK* *ACK*
<Mimi> hey renard :)
<Hyker> i got new ones last week
<Mimi> smug: hehe..you seem like it..I'm alright :) on SB finally ;)
<smug> i talk3 lines at a time
<le_renard> The author said the french version translates to "Internet
           for Zeroes".
<poop> see ya
*** IRCDough:          Chn: #nicecafe %+     18:51
```

Notice the abbreviations, exaggerated spelling (grrreat), and smilies. This is typical of IRC. Indeed, some groups are hard to decipher because of shared language conventions.

WHERE CAN YOU GET MORE INFORMATION ABOUT IRC?

An FTP site, **cs.ftp.bu.edu,** offers client software for IRC and tutorials in the /irc/support directory, as well as other information such as a list of servers that offer Telnet access to IRC.

Some USENET newsgroups focus on IRC. The most generic is **alt.irc,** which also offers a FAQ (frequently asked questions). There are also more specific newsgroups oriented around certain IRC channels.

WHAT IS A MUD?

A MUD (Multiple-User Dungeon) is one of many names for a whole category of communication utilities that offer CHAT-like conversation in an interactive fictional environment. Each user (or mudder) assumes a computerized persona or character and, via textual descriptions, can move through settings, talk with other characters, and solve puzzles. Mudders can even create rooms, items, and their own descriptions. Most MUDs are based on a specific theme, such as cyberspace, medieval kingdoms, or interstellar empires, and users are expected to assume characters consistent with the theme.

There are many subcategories of MUDs, such as TinyMUDs, LP-MUDs, MUCKs, MUSHes, MUSEs, and MOOs. TinyMUD players gather to chat, meet friends, and socialize in a fictional setting; LP-MUDs are generally based on role-playing adventure games and are usually jam-packed with monsters to slay and riddles to decipher, creating a much more goal-oriented environment.

While most MUDs are recreational, some are educational, used by secondary and university classes for students to communicate with other students from around the country and the world. Educators have found that the real-time synchronous communication, the blending of play with work, and the opportunities for interaction with distant students break down traditional barriers of a class setting. Students enjoy the game-like qualities and anonymity of MUDs and often feel more comfortable expressing themselves in the MUD environment than they do in a traditional classroom. Students, as they discuss topics related to their classes, also learn how to manipulate the MUD environment.

HOW DO YOU ACCESS A MUD?

You can connect to a MUD's Internet port via Telnet or a specific client program designed for MUDs. A client MUD program is preferable to Telnet because it provides a smoother interface, allowing, for example, advanced word wrap, which prevents words of different characters from being intermingled. If you have a SLIP or PPP connection, you may be able to install a MUD client program on your computer. If you are connecting through a lab or dial-up connection to a time-sharing computer network, you are probably restricted to Telnet, unless someone at the university takes a strong interest in MUDs and has installed a MUD client on the university network.

After you connect to a MUD, you will see a welcome screen which gives basic information such as what to type to begin a session. Most MUDs allow a new user to create a persona and dive right in; however, some require you to submit a request for a new character via e-mail. When you log on, read the screen carefully for instructions on how to begin. It may also be helpful to read the on-line help once you are connected to a MUD, by typing **help** at the MUD's command prompt. Along with your new character, you will be asked to specify a password, which prevents unauthorized users from using your character in the MUD.

Commands can vary significantly from one MUD to another, but generally there are commands that allow users to move from location to location within the fictional setting of the MUD and a set of CHAT-like commands that allow users to communicate through both public and person-to-person messages. Some MUDs even allow users to add to the environment and story line, creating new places to explore, greater depth and detail in existing settings, and carefully worded character descriptions which bring the MUD to life. These story-building commands are usually prefaced by a **@.**

SOME TYPICAL MUD COMMANDS

help	Generates help screen
news	Displays announcements
look	Shows room description
look <object>	Displays object description
@describe me (*or* **@desc me**)	Sets your description
go (direction, place)	Moves you to another room
say (your comments)	Displays your comment
act (action)	Expresses action
who	Shows other players
quit	Ends

FOR MORE INFORMATION ABOUT MUDs

World Wide Web sites for MUD information include **http://aragorn.uio.no/** and **http://www.cis.upenn.edu/~lwl/mudinfo.html.** The second site offers a searchable list of MUDs. You can also obtain a list of MUDs by sending a message to Peter Wozniak at **awozniak@geordi.calpoly.edu.** For the most recent issue of his list, send the message **ISSUE** in the subject line of your e-mail message (his automated program looks only at the subject line, not the message space). An FAQ (Frequently Asked Questions) about MUDs is posted to **rec.games.mud.announce** and is also available via FTP from **ftp.math.okstate.edu:pub/muds/misc/ mud.faq.** This FTP site also offers other documents about MUDs, as does **ftp.tcp.com** and **parcftp.xerox.com:/pub/Moo/.** The FAQ is also available at

**gopher.physics.utoronto.ca:/USENETNewsFrequentlyAskedQuestions(FAQ)/
rec./Rec.games.mud: FAQ*.** Several USENET newsgroups are dedicated to MUDs,
including these:

rec.games.mud.announce	Information on MUDs
rec.games.mud.mis	Miscellaneous aspects of MUDs
rec.games.mud.admin	Administrative issues

A SAMPLE ACADEMIC MOO

CollegeTown is an academic MOO (MUD Object Oriented) which is open to students. It can be reached by Telnet at **patty.bvu.edu.** CollegeTown is set in a small
college town in the scenic countryside. The mission: provide a platform for academic research and learning. This is done through an expanded classroom environment including everything from walks on the beach and a trek up Mount Lothar to
a small city to explore.

   Connect to CollegeTown and you will receive this welcoming screen.

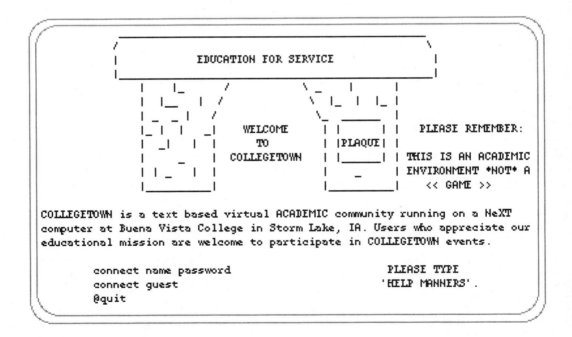

Type **connect guest** and you will be transported to the guest lounge.

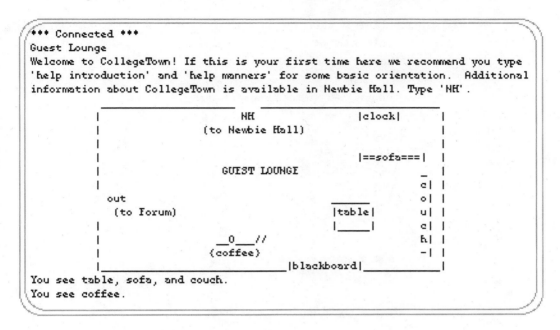

```
*** Connected ***
Guest Lounge
Welcome to CollegeTown! If this is your first time here we recommend you type
'help introduction' and 'help manners' for some basic orientation.  Additional
information about CollegeTown is available in Newbie Hall. Type 'NH'.
    _____
         |                        NH                  |clock|      |
         |                   (to Newbie Hall)                       |
         |                                                          |
         |                                            |==sofa===|   |
         |                  GUEST LOUNGE                   _        |
         |                                                c|        |
      out        |                              _____    o|        |
       (to Forum)                              |table|    u|        |
         |                                     |_____|    c|        |
         |                  __O___ //                     h|        |
         |                  (coffee)                      -|        |
         |_____|blackboard|_____ |
You see table, sofa, and couch.
You see coffee.
```

From here you can begin your exploration of the interactive CollegeTown environment. The top of this screen instructs you to type both **help introduction** and **help manners** for basic information on life in CollegeTown. After you have read the introductory material, take a while to explore this new world. You may even be able to strike up a conversation with someone on the nature trail. When you are finished, type **@quit** to exit CollegeTown and return to your system.

A FEW MUDs AND MOOs

Listed below is a sampling of MUDs and MOOs. To connect to a MUD or MOO, type **telnet** (address) (port), leaving a space between the address and the port number.

CollegeTown MOO
        Host: **patty.bvu.edu**
        Port: 7777
        Theme: educational

The Cruel and Lost World of Stonia
> Host: **madli.ut.ee**
> Numeric: 193.40.5.124
> Port: 4000
> Theme: research/social/talker/fantasy

The Glass Dragon
> Host: **surf.tstc.edu**
> Numeric: 161.109.32.2
> Port: 4000
> Theme: social/fantasy

Kerovnia
> Host: **atlantis.edu**
> Numeric: 192.67.238.48
> Port: 1984
> Theme: social/talker/fantasy/sci-fi

LambdaMOO
> Host: **lambda.xerox.com**
> Numeric: 192.216.54.2
> Port: 8888
> Theme: educational/social

Midnight Sun
> Host: **midnight-sun.ludd.luth.se**
> Numeric: 130.240.16.23
> Port: 3000
> Theme: social/fantasy

ASSIGNMENTS

1. Connect to IRC and explore several channels. Report to your small group about the conversations that took place.
2. Explore two MUDs, learning the basic commands. Report to your small group what you experienced.
3. Write a review of one MUD, including basic commands and a description of the activity.
4. Contact another user with the TALK utility. Write a short comparison of TALK and e-mail communication.

QUESTIONS TO ASK

1. How do you access the TALK utility with your Internet connection?
2. Does your university support a CHAT program? If so, how do you access it?
3. Does your university offer an IRC connection? If so, how do you access it?
4. Are there any restrictions on IRC or MUD usage (some universities restrict use to certain hours, others do not allow these at all)?
5. Does your university computer network offer a MUD client? If so, what are the basic commands?

PART THREE

SEARCHING
FOR INFORMATION

SEVEN

WORLD WIDE WEB

The World Wide Web, often abbreviated WWW, W3, or Web, is a powerful new way to explore Internet resources. It is an innovative hypertext/hypermedia system which allows you to follow facts, ideas, and texts from one hypertext link to another, taking as many nonlinear steps as you like. What does that mean? Let's begin by defining hypertext and hypermedia.

Hypertext is information stored in a nonhierarchical structure in which each piece of hypertext is connected to one or more other pieces of hypertext by links. Anyone who has ever followed a cross-reference in a dictionary has used a primitive form of hypertext. If you look up the word *kaleyard* in the dictionary, for example, you may find that after the definition there is a "see also" reference (see also: kitchen garden). If you look up *kitchen garden*, you will find related information. You will have also followed a primitive hypertext link. Hypertext becomes tremendously powerful when implemented electronically. A computerized hypertext document allows you simply to click on a link to follow it. From the new document, you may wish to follow another link, then another, eventually creating a web of links that you have followed to find the information you are looking for. At any point in the process you can back up to a previous link and explore other hypertext paths.

Hypermedia refers to data that are not purely textual but include images and/or sound. This digital sensory bazaar is especially exciting for computer users accustomed to character-based screen displays. World Wide Web pages look more like glossy magazine features than like text displays from other Internet protocols such as gopher or FTP.

One of the primary goals of WWW is to provide simple, straightforward access to all on-line knowledge, not merely WWW documents, although there are millions of those. The unique hypertext format of the Web has evolved to allow simple access to FTP sites, gopher menus, WAIS search engines, USENET newsgroups, and all the millions of resources to which those protocols provide access. These nonweb documents may not be hypertext or hypermedia, but they are linked in the Web to related documents.

WWW can also be used for two-way communication. Through WWW forms, the user can be asked questions, a capability that can be used for everything from ordering pizza to joining interest groups. Because it is so adaptable, powerful, and easy to use, the World Wide Web is possibly the fastest growing of the Internet tools. With the WWW you can browse an electronic art gallery, obtain the newest version of your favorite software, or go shopping for a new mountain bike. With a good connection and good browsing software, you may find it simpler to do all of your Internet work through the WWW. That's right. Instead of using the procedures for FTP, gopher, and Telnet (discussed in later chapters), you can operate all of these protocols through the Web.

This chapter will demonstrate how to access the World Wide Web through two different programs, one making use of hypermedia and the other text-based. Then it will illustrate how to find WWW resources through a key-word search engine.

WHAT ARE WEB PAGES?

World Wide Web is made up of documents called pages, which combine images, text, and even sound. A home page is the entry point for users to access a collection of pages. Certain words, images, or icons on each page act as links to other WWW pages. By clicking on a linked word, image, or icon, you can jump to other pages, which may be stored on the same server or on another one on the other side of the world. Location is unimportant; the software will locate and retrieve the information. The user only has to tell it which links to follow.

When you select a link on a WWW page, you are actually telling a scripted computer program to access the data. Most pages are preformatted in HTML (HyperText Markup Language) with embedded pointers which tell the browser where to find the linked pages. Other pages are created as you access them through an automated process. And with some extra software, it is possible to create your own hypertext documents and link them to the Web.

WHAT ARE BROWSERS?

The World Wide Web is accessed through client programs called browsers, which allow you to browse through documents and explore links to other documents at the same or other sites. These browsers exist on three different levels from line mode to full graphic interface, allowing you to use as sophisticated a browser as your Internet connection and software will support. The following are the three levels, listed in descending order of sophistication:

1. Mosaic, Netscape, or other full graphic interface will display hypertext and hypermedia documents with text in a variety of fonts, colors, and sizes. To use one of these sophisticated browsers, you need to use a lab computer with the browser installed, or you must have a SLIP or PPP connection for your home computer.

2. Lynx is a full-screen interface, but without graphics. Text is arranged in menus that look somewhat like gopher (see Chapter 8), but you move through them by selecting links rather than menu items. You may find Lynx installed on your university's system, or you can access it by telneting to a site such as **lynx.cc.ukans.edu** (log in as **WWW**).

3. Simple WWW line browsers do not have a graphic interface and are less than user friendly because they show only part of a screen at a time. You can try one by telnetting to **telnet.W3.ORG.** You would probably want to try Lynx or a full graphic interface first, if possible.

The ideal connection to WWW would be a full graphic interface such as Mosaic or Netscape running on a fast computer, because it would enable you to appreciate all the wonderful graphics and sound available and to explore links with a simple click of the mouse. At some universities access to Mosaic or Netscape is limited to networked computers in labs, and dial-in users must use Lynx. More and more universities, however, offer PPP or SLIP connections which support dial-in connections for graphic browsers.

If you don't have access to a full-featured browser, you can still reach the same documents through Lynx, but you just won't have the graphics and sound. Many documents accessible through WWW, including most FTP and gopher documents, do not contain any graphics or sound, and so the less sophisticated browsers may provide just as much information as a powerful graphical browser would. However, many WWW sites have begun to take advantage of the innovations made possible by graphical browsers, and some documents with graphics make little or no sense unless viewed with a graphically-oriented browser.

WWW ADDRESSES

Browsing through the Web and selecting links to explore is one of the ways to get to pages within the WWW. Another way to reach a page is to input locations directly. Locations on the Web are referenced by Uniform Resource Locators (URLs). URLs are addresses made up of long and cryptic-appearing strings of letters which can be used to describe any Internet resource. When you are browsing through WWW, you usually do not need to know a page's URL because that information is embedded into the hypertext link. However, if there is a site you wish to access and you don't want to have to pass through several links to get there, you can submit its URL directly and move there immediately. For example, here is the address of a page that provides an introduction to WWW.

```
http://info.cern.ch/hypertext/WWW/Talks/General/
Concepts.html
```

Let's go through the address one step at a time. The first section of a URL shows the type of information being accessed. In this case **http** means that the document is in hypertext format (see "Other Internet Protocols" below for examples of other types of information). The **://** is a divider, followed by **info.cern.ch,** the host name of the site where the document is stored. At this point some URLs would also include a port number. The standard port number for WWW is 80, and it is not usually necessary to include it when submitting a URL; however, some servers may require this additional information. The next section, **/hypertext/WWW/Talks/ General/,** is the directory path to where the page is stored. Finally, **Concepts. html** is the filename that the page is stored under at the host.

HOW DO YOU USE WWW?

You begin by accessing your WWW browser, be it Lynx, Mosaic, or whatever. You will be connected to your home page, that is, to the first hypertext page your browser accesses whenever you run it. The home page may be one constructed or selected by your university system or the default one established by the people who wrote your browser. From there you follow the colored (highlighted on some browsers) links to other sites or documents. On the Netscape home page, for example, links are provided to several help documents, including a guided tour of the Internet, a list of what's new in WWW sites, and a FAQ (Frequently Asked Questions). Simply click on the colored word that interests you, and you will be connected to the linked document. Once the page is displayed, you can scroll through it by using your mouse to control the slider at the bottom or right side of the page just as you would in any Windows or Mac document.

Basic functions included with all of the graphical browsers include the ability to move "back" to the previous page, "forward" to return to a link after moving back, and "home" to allow you to return to your home page. Each program also has a means for you to access any particular WWW site directly. In Netscape, for example, if you want to access a particular hypertext site or document, you click on the **Open** button at the top of the screen and type in the appropriate URL in the dialogue box that opens. In Mosaic you select **Open URL** from the **File** menu. Finally, most browsers have a "hotlist" or "bookmark" option. When you find a resource on the WWW that seems useful, you can save the URL as a bookmark, eventually creating a list of your favorite Web pages and enabling you to return to them easily.

OTHER INTERNET PROTOCOLS

While browsing through the WWW, you may run across pages that are slightly reformatted gopher menus or directory listings from FTP sites. WWW browsers can also be used to access these Internet resources directly. All you have to do is submit the URL for the resource you wish to access. Recall that the URLs begin with the name of the type of information being accessed. For example, the following are the basic formats of the URLs for gopher, FTP, Telnet, and USENET resources, respectively:

```
gopher://(address)
ftp://(address)
telnet://(address)
news:(name-of-group)
```

Accessing FTP through WWW offers the same advantages as does gopher FTP: menu access and the ability to read files without retrieving them. For the other protocols, it simply allows you to retrieve files from a site without leaving your WWW browser.

CREATING WEB PAGES

The World Wide Web makes world-wide publishing possible to anyone who is able to arrange disk space on a server and has some basic knowledge of how pages are created. Students at an increasing number of universities are creating World Wide Web pages as part of class projects. Some pages are personal, giving information about the individual and even including a photo. Others are subject-oriented, publishing papers written in a particular class.

In order to publish on the World Wide Web, you need to know basic HTML (hypertext markup language). HTML documents which translate into Web pages when placed on a server have two components: text written in plain text (ASCII) and HTML tags that indicate document structure, formatting, and hypertext links to other documents. A HTML tag indicating a heading, for example, would look like this:

```
<H1>Creating Web Pages</H1>
```

The information between the less than (<) and the greater than (>) symbols tells a Web browser such as Netscape or Mosaic how to display the text. These are toggle tags which tell the browser to turn the heading display on and off, so a tag is required before the text and one (with a / symbol) after the text.

HTML documents can be created in any word processing program and converted to ASCII. Or you can use any of a number of HTML editors available as freeware or for purchase. The HTML editors relieve you of the necessity of learning the HTML language. If you want a heading of a certain size or bold face type, you use pull-down menus to select your option, and the editor creates the HTML tags for you.

The World Wide Web itself has a wealth of documents on how to create Web pages. The following pages have links to a number of documents and places where you can download freeware HTML editors.

```
A Beginner's Guide to HTML
http://www.ncsa.uiuc.edu/demoweb/html-primer.html
HTML Documentation
http://www.utirc.utoronto.ca/HTMLdocs/NewHTML/htmlindex.
html
The Repository
http://cbl.leeds.ac.uk/nikos/doc/repository.html
Yahoo
http://www.yahoo.com/Computers/
World_Wide_Web/
```

A SESSION USING A GRAPHICAL BROWSER

The powerful graphically oriented browsers are the windows through which the Web is truly designed to be viewed.

If you are using Netscape for the Macintosh, for example, you would begin by double-clicking on the Netscape icon on your program manager screen. You would then be connected to your home page. Once you have your home page loaded, you can begin to explore the links it offers or submit a URL to the browser directly. For this example, begin by submitting the URL for the White House. That's right, the home of the President of the United States can now be visited on-line. The URL for the White House is **http://www.whitehouse.gov.** The process for submitting a URL directly will vary from browser to browser. Netscape has a button labeled **open.** When you click on the button, the browser opens a window where you can type in the URL to which you wish to connect.

When you reach the White House Web site, you will be greeted with the home page that appears on page 79. This page can be broken down into individual components. The top portion of the display is browser specific for the Macintosh Netscape, so it may not look exactly like your screen if you are using another browser. This top section contains buttons allowing easy access to some of the more useful functions of the browser. Below these buttons is the window where hypertext pages are displayed. In this case it contains the main page for the White House site. Now that you have this picture of the White House, surrounded by some text and smaller pictures, what do you do with it?

Each of the graphics on this page is a graphical hypertext link to other pages. To connect to another page, all you have to do is click on the item in which you are interested. For example, if you were taking a government class and had to do a paper about the office of the Secretary of Education, you might begin to search for information at the White House site. The Secretary of Education is a member of the President's Cabinet, which is part of the Executive

Branch of government. In order to find out more about the Executive Branch, you would click on this graphic:

which is located just to the left of the picture of the White House. Your browser will follow the hypertext link and display the following page:

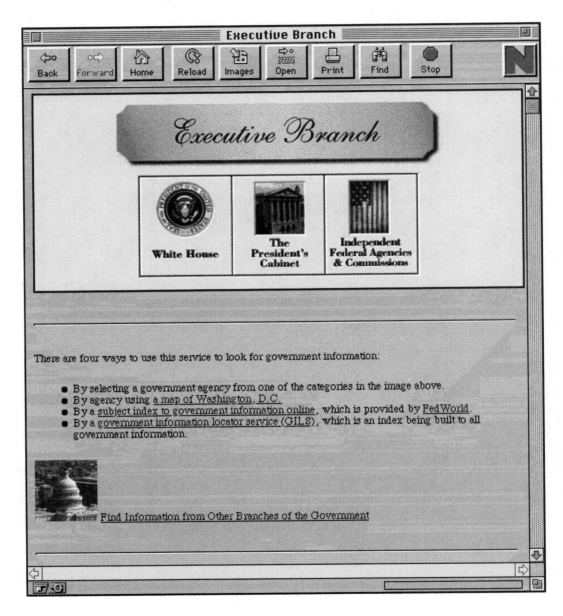

This page begins with a graphic, under which is some text. Some of the text is underlined and highlighted. The underlined text is a hypertext link. When you read the line, "•By agency using a map of Washington, D.C." you can click on the underlined portion to access a page containing a map of Washington, D.C.

To continue your exploration, look at the graphic in the upper portion of the screen. You are interested in information about the President's Cabinet, so you would click on the corresponding picture. Your browser will access the following page:

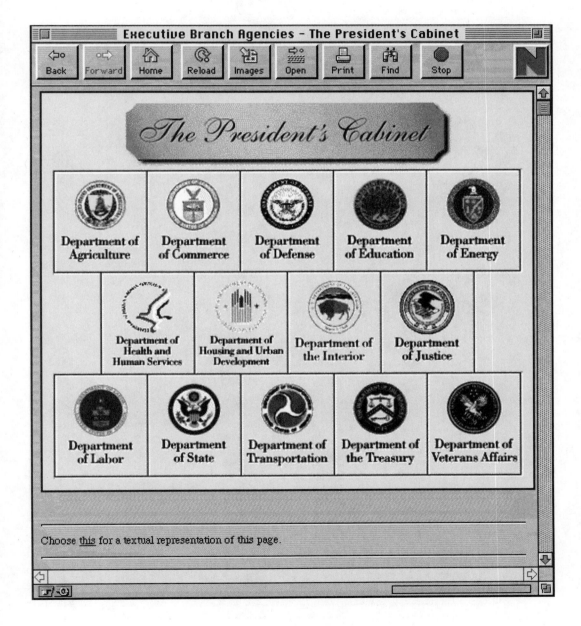

The pictures on this page are graphical hypertext links to information about each of the posts in the President's Cabinet. In order to find information about the Secretary of Education, click on the

graphic. This will connect you to the Department of Education page, shown below:

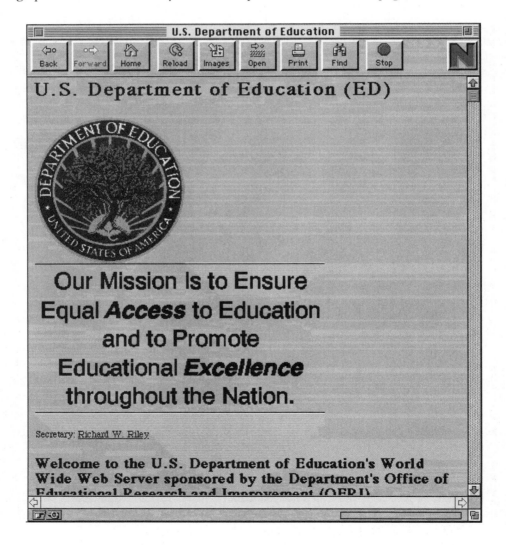

This is the page you have been looking for! Scrolling through this page, you will find information about the Cabinet post, the department, and its mission. The page also contains a number of hypertext links to other pages, including a short biography page about the current Secretary of Education. You could print a copy of the biography by simply going to the **Print** button at the top of the screen, or you could copy the text to a disk by going to the **File** menu at the top of the screen of the Macintosh (not reproduced here) and select **Save As.** At any point you can use the **Back** and **Forward** buttons to explore hypertext links to other parts of the White House Web pages.

SAMPLE LYNX SESSION

Lynx is a browser that supports full-screen, text-only connection to the WWW. It is installed on many university local networks and, at the time of publication, was accessible via Telnet at the University of Kansas, **lynx.cc.ukans.edu.** Because Lynx is not an option on every university system, this example uses the option of telnetting to the University of Kansas. If you are not familiar with Telnet, refer to Chapter 10. This first screen welcomes you to the university.

```
www.cc.ukans.edu default index

WELCOME TO THE UNIVERSITY OF KANSAS

You are using a World–Wide Web client called Lynx on a server operated by Academic Computing
Services at the University of Kansas, which is the home of

        *        KUfacts, the KU campus wide information system, and

        *        the Lynx and DosLynx World–Wide Web (WWW) browsers.

The current version of Lynx is 2.3.  If you are running an earlier version PLEASE UPGRADE!

The Lynx 2–3–1 source code is now available for BETA testing.

INFORMATION SOURCES ABOUT AND FOR THE WWW
        * For a description of the WWW choose Web Overview
        * About the WWW Information Sharing project
        * WWW Information by Subject

—press space for next page—
        Arrow keys: Up an Down to move.  Right to follow a link; Left to go back.
H)elp O)ptions P)rint G)o M)ain screen Q)uit?=search [delete]=history list

129.108.1.4
```

A number of words on this screen are hypertext links to other documents. Let's go browsing. For a new user, the option "For a description of the WWW choose Web Overview" might be informative. Choose it and you will receive this screen.

WWW ICON GENERAL OVERVIEW OF THE WEB

There is no "top" to the World—Wide Web. You can look at it from many points of view. Here are some places to start.

Virtual Library by Subject
　　　　The Virtual Library organizes information by subject matter.

List of servers
　　　　All registered HTTP servers by country

by Service Type
　　　　　　　　The Web includes data accessible by many other
　　　　　　　　protocols. The lists by access protocol may help if
　　　　　　　　you know what kind of service you are looking
　　　　　　　　for.

If you find a useful starting point for you personally, you can configure your WWW browser to start there by default.

—press space for next page—
　　　　Arrow keys: Up an Down to move. Right to follow a link; Left to go back.
H)elp O)ptions P)rint G)o M)ain screen Q)uit?=search [delete]=history list

129.108.1.4

This screen gives you several options, including "Virtual Library by Subject." A virtual library could be a useful tool, both for research and recreation. Selecting that link leads to the following screen, which gives a little information about the Virtual Library.

The World—Wide Web Virtual Library: Subject Catalog (p I of 14)

VIRTUAL LIBRARY THE WWW VIRTUAL LIBRARY

This is a distributed subject catalog. See Category Subtree, Library of Congress Classification (Experimental), Top Ten most popular Fields (Experimental), Statistics (Experimental), and Index. See also arrangement by service type., and other subject catalogs of network information.

```
Mail to maintainers of the specified subject or www-request@mail.W3.org to add pointer to this
list, or if you would like to contribute to administration of a subject area.

See also how to put your data on the web.   All items starting with ! are NEW! (or newly
maintained).   New this month: [INLINE] Electronic Journals [INLINE] Finance [INLINE] Human Rights
[INLINE] Medieval Studies [INLINE]

Aboriginal Studies
        This document keeps track of leading information facilities
—press space for next page—
        Arrow keys: Up an Down to move.  Right to follow a link; Left to go back.
H)elp O)ptions P)rint G)o M)ain screen Q)uit?=search [delete]=history list

129.108.1.4
```

One of the options on the Virtual Library page above is "Category Subtree." Select it and Lynx will retrieve this screen showing the first few items in the subject list.

```
              The World-Wide Web Virtual Library:   Subject Catalog (p 2 of 10)

* Alternative Science
        + Paranormal Phenomena
        + Unidentified Flying Objects (UFOs)
* Animal health, wellbeing, and rights
* Anthropology
        + Aboriginal Studies
* Archaeology
* Architecture
        + Landscape Architecture
* Bio Sciences
        + Biochemistry
        + Biodiversity and Ecology
        + Biological Molecules
        + Entomology
        + Evolution
        + Fish
        + Genetics
        + Herpetology
        + Medicine
                o Anesthesiology
```

—press space for next page—
        Arrow keys: Up an Down to move. Right to follow a link; Left to go back.
H)elp O)ptions P)rint G)o M)ain screen Q)uit?=search [delete]=history list

129.108.1.4

From here you might take a look at "Archaeology" and see what the Virtual Library has to offer. The next screen gives you several options.

Archaeological Regions

                            Internet   resources by geographic region.
                            Email archnet@spirit.lib.uconn.edu if you
                            would like to register your WWW server or
                            know of online information not in these lists.

        Updated: 11/21/94

        * Africa * Asia * Australia and Pacific * Central America

        * Europe * Near East * North America * South America

        [Africa] [Asia] [Southeast Asia] [Central America] [Europe]
        [Near East] [North America] [South America]

—press space for next page—
        Arrow keys: Up an Down to move. Right to follow a link; Left to go back.
H)elp O)ptions P)rint G)o M)ain screen Q)uit?=search [delete]=history list

129.108.1.4

This screen divides archaeology into regions of the world. North American Archaeology might be interesting. Let's explore it.

```
                                    ArchNet: Regions/North America (p 1 of 4)

Internet Resources for North American Archaeology
        [INLINE}

        _____

                        Internet    resources    related    to    the
                        archaeology  of  North  America.   Click here
                        to register a new server.


        Updated: 2/14/95

        _____


                        * Archaeology of the Northeastern United
                        States — University of Connecticut

                        * Canadian Heritage Information Network

                        * Ecolab Gopher: Archaeology of the
                        Southeastern United States—University of
                        Georgia


—press space for next page—
        Arrow keys: Up an Down to move.  Right to follow a link; Left to go back.
H)elp O)ptions P)rint G)o M)ain screen Q)uit?=search [delete]=history list

129.108.1.4
```

The Virtual Library offers three options in North American Archaeology. Let's take a look at the first selection, "Archaeology of the Northeastern United States," which is stored at the University of Connecticut.

```
                                    Northeastern United States (p 1 of 4)

Northeastern Archaeology

              _____

                        Reports, data, and images related to the
                        prehistoric and historic archaeology of the
                        northeastern United States.  Many of the
                        sources listed below are cross indexed in
                        other portions of ArchNet.

              Updated: 1/25/95

ARTIFACT CATALOGS

        *The Prehistoric Ceramics of Southern New England.

        * A Guide to New England Projectile Points.

        *The Bull Collection.

—press space for next page—
          Arrow keys: Up an Down to move.  Right to follow a link; Left to go back.
H)elp O)ptions P)rint G)o M)ain screen Q)uit?=search [delete]=history list

129.108.1.4
```

Here we see that the University of Connecticut features several archaeological collections. Again, choose the first one, "The Prehistoric Ceramics of Southern New
England."

Virtual Catalog of Prehistoric Ceramics

[INLINE}

A catalog of Windsor Tradition ceramics from southern New England. In this region, Windsor is the local indigenous ceramic tradition, with dates ranging between ca. 3,000 and 300 Years BP.

For each type listed below there are illustrations, descriptions, and references to archaeological site reports. The list presented below is arranged in chronological order with the earlier types appearing at the top.

Compiled by Jon Lizee with illustrations by Tara Prindle and hypertext by Tom Plunkett.

The Windsor Ceramic Tradition
—press space for next page—
        Arrow keys: Up an Down to move. Right to follow a link; Left to go back.
H)elp O)ptions P)rint G)o M)ain screen Q)uit?=search [delete]=history list

129.108.1.4

A virtual catalogue for ceramics! This may not be terrifically exiting to a math major, but it could be valuable to someone studying archaeology and it demonstrates the depth of information available on the World Wide Web. In fact, looking down this page, you will find that there are also illustrations available in this exhibit. Because this is Lynx rather than a graphical browser like Netscape, you cannot see the illustrations, although you can still read the text descriptions.

Lynx can be a powerful tool if you are looking for text information. It is relatively fast, because no time is spent loading graphics. It can be frustrating, however, not to be able to see graphics accompanying a text. Also, Lynx sites sometimes have the **Go** option disabled which means that you cannot enter the address of a specific WWW site. If that is the case, you can only follow hypertext links to sites. This greatly restricts your Web explorations.

HOW DO YOU FIND WWW SITES?

The World Wide Web is a fast-growing and valuable resource for information on a wide range of topics from aircraft to zoology, but you have to be able to locate the information to use it. There are several avenues open to you:

1. Use the hypertext links. Begin at your home page and explore the highlighted links to sites such as the Virtual Library and see what you find. In order to appreciate the resources available through the WWW you need to spend some time browsing Web pages. As you find pages which may be helpful to you in the future, you can add them to your bookmark list.
2. Become familiar with topic-oriented sites which offer links to other sites. A number of these are listed at the end of this chapter.
3. Use index books such as *New Riders' Official World Wide Web Yellow Pages* which list WWW sites by topic.
4. Take advantage of the WWW search engines which provide free key-word searches of sites.

WWW SEARCH ENGINES

The hypertext content of Web documents complicates key-word indexing. A number of search engines (sometimes called spiders) are able to use the structure of HTML to look for topical information in headings and hypertext links marked by HTML tags. What the search engines offer is a rating of Web documents and sites according to how many times the word or phrase you specify appears in a document or list of site documents. You may need to try two or three different search engines to find information about your topic because they index different sites in somewhat different ways.

SEARCH ENGINE DEMONSTRATION—WEBCRAWLER

To access one of the WWW search engines, you can use a hypertext link if your home page offers links to a variety of search engines. If not, you can use the **Open** or **Open URL** feature of Netscape or other browser to connect to the specific address of a search engine. The following demonstration uses WebCrawler. A list of search engines is provided in a box which follows the demonstration.

Suppose you are using a freeware version of the e-mail program Eudora which is provided by your university. Many of the features are self-explanatory, but you would like to learn about some of the more sophisticated options Eudora offers. You can use a WWW search engine to locate information about Eudora. Connect to WebCrawler at the address **http://webcrawler.cs.washington.edu/ WebCrawler/Home.html.** You will receive this screen:

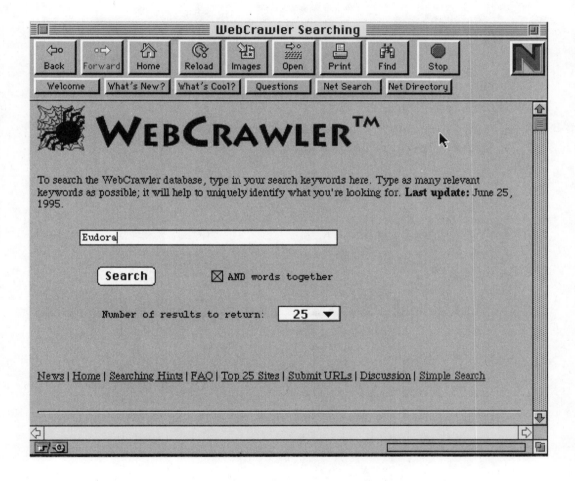

Note that the word **Eudora** has already been typed into the box provided for key words. You can type in whichever key word or words will specify your search topic. After you type your word or words, click on the **Search** button. After a moment or two, the search engine will provide a list of documents or sites which have a high frequency of using your key word or words. A list of documents or sites with information about **Eudora** follows:

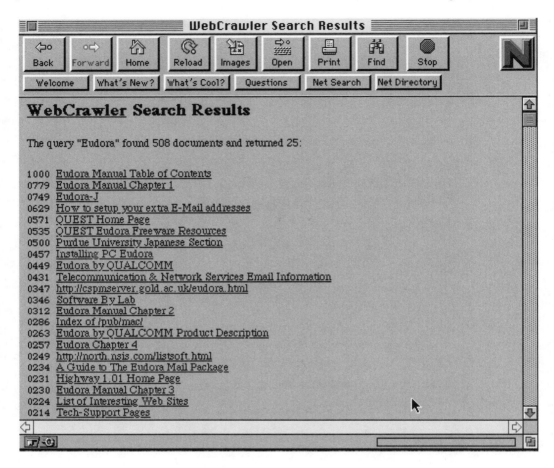

Looking through this list, several items look like they might offer information about using Eudora. For example, if you highlight "A Guide to the Eudora Mail Package" and press enter, you will see one college's on-line manual for Eudora. As always with search engine results, you do not really know what you are accessing until you call up the text. It is a trial and error process, though a little effort will usually result in information about your topic.

LIST OF WORLD WIDE WEB SEARCH ENGINES

ALIWEB	http://web.nexor.co.uk/public/aliweb/aliweb.html
Lycos	http://lycos.cs.cmu.edu
Jumpstation	http://www.stir.ac.uk/jsbin/js
Web Nomad	http://www.rns.com/www_index/intro.html
W3 Search Engine	shttp://cuiwww.unige.ch/meta-index.html
WebCrawler	http://webcrawler.com Crawler/Home.html
WWW Worm	http://www.cs.colorado.edu/home/mcbryan/ WWWW.html

SOME INTERESTING WWW PAGES

The following Web pages offer rich collections of documents and also links to other collections. To access them, open your browser and type the address in your **Open** or **Open URL** dialogue box.

A Beginner's Guide to HTML
```
http://www.ncsa.uiuc.edu/demoweb/html-primer.html
```
American Universities
```
http://www.clas.ufl.edu/CLAS/american-universities.
html
```
The Awesome List
```
http://www.clark.net/pub/journalism/awesome.html
```
E-Zine-List (list of on-line magazines)
```
http://www.meer.net/~johnl/e-zine-list/index.html
```
Global Network Navigator
```
http://nearnet.gnn.com/gnn/gnn.html
```
Guide to the Web
```
http://www.hcc.hawaii.edu/guide/www.guide.html
```
Internet Resources Meta-Index
```
http://www.ncsa.uiuc.edu/SDG/Software/Mosaic/
MetaIndex.html
```
Library of Congress
```
http://lcweb.loc.gov
```

List of WWW Servers—CERN

> http://info.cern.ch/hypertext/DataSources/WWW/
> Servers.html

Museums

> http://www-external.hal.com/pages/hops.html#Museums
> http://www.comlab.ox.ac.uk/archive/other/
> museums.html

Newspaper and Journalism Links

> http://www.spub.ksu.edu/other/journ.html

Nova-Links

> http://www.nova.edu/Inter-Links

Open Market (business Web sites)

> http://www.openmarket.com

Sports

> http://www.atm.ch.cam.ac.uk/sports/sports.html

ESPN SportsZone

> http://espnet.sportszone.com

U.S. Federal Agencies

> http://www.lib.lsu.edu/gov/fedgov.html
> http://www.fedworld.gov

Vatican Exhibit

> http://sunsite.unc.edu/expo/vatican.exhibit
> /Vatican.exhibit.html

Virtual Tourist World Map

> http://wings.buffalo.edu/world

White House

> http://www.whitehouse.gov

The Whole Internet Catalog

> http://nearnet.gnn.com/wic/newrescat.toc.html

Who's Who on the Internet

> http://web.city.ac.uk/citylive/pages.html

World Lecture Hall (class materials)

> http://wwwhost.cc.utexas.edu/world/instruction/
> index.html

World Wide Web Home

> http://www.w3.org

WWW Virtual Library

> http://www.w3.org/hypertext/DataSources/bySubject

Yahoo (subject index)

> http://www.yahoo.com

ASSIGNMENTS

1. Access the Virtual Library, explore it, and write a memo about the materials available there.
2. Access the Virtual Library and download one text from it.
3. Browsing through the World Wide Web, compile a list of ten sites which interest you. Share these with your small group.
4. Write a review of a World Wide Web site, including its purpose, range of materials, and target audience.
5. Using one of the Web search engines, search for a topic related to your major. Compile a list of Web sites and explore them. Write an annotated bibliography of the sites.

QUESTIONS TO ASK

1. Does your university support PPP or SLIP connections to the Internet? If so, does it make WWW software such as Netscape or Mosaic available to students?
2. Is Lynx or another WWW browser installed on the university time-sharing network, if there is one? If so, how do you access it?
3. Do the computers in the lab(s) on your campus have Netscape, Mosaic, or other graphical browsers?

EIGHT

GOPHER AND VERONICA

WHAT IS GOPHER?

Gopher is a curious but perhaps not inappropriate name for an extremely useful computer application which provides menu access to Internet resources. A gopher, by definition, is (1) a burrowing rodent of North and Central America belonging to the family Geomyidae or (2) a zealously eager assistant who runs errands. The computer application Gopher is both. It burrows through the Internet finding desired information, and it runs errands seeking pathways to interconnecting databases around the world. And it does this in a way that provides simple, easy-to-use menus for information retrieval.

Gopher is an information browsing service, which means that it enables users to find, examine, and download information stored on remote computers. It is a "client/server" protocol, meaning that the user accesses "client" gopher software which, with a few commands, will establish a connection with a remote computer running "server" gopher software that enables the user to explore and download information from the server database.

WHAT CAN YOU FIND WITH GOPHER?

Gopher provides easy access to a huge number of resources located all over the world. Through gopher you can gain access to electronic books, journals, and reference materials; searchable databases, library catalogs, images, sounds, artwork, and music; job listings, phone books, financial aid information, course schedules, university calendars, up to the minute news and weather; personal computer software, government documents, movie reviews, access to freenets and public bulletin board system sites; and thousands of other resources. Gopher presents the Internet as an organized directory system, like the directories on a DOS machine or folders on a Macintosh. While gopher does not have hypertext links as does the World Wide Web, it does offer links through menu items to related gopher menus at other sites.

HOW DO YOU USE GOPHER?

Different universities offer different options for using gopher. As with most Internet protocols, the options for gopher are affected by the type of connection available to the user. Gopher access can be divided into five basic types.

1. Networked personal computers, often available in campus computer labs, offer fast and easy-to-use access. Turbogopher and GopherApp for the Mac, or Winsock Gopher and PC Gopher for the PC, are some of the more common programs which allow simple point-and-click access to gopher menus from networked machines.
2. Universities that offer SLIP or PPP dial-up services make it possible to use the same software packages mentioned in type 1 from home computers with a modem.
3. Access to the above type connections means you can access the World Wide Web via a graphical browser such as Netscape or Mosaic. As was discussed in Chapter 7, the WWW also displays gopher sites.
4. Some universities provide a menu-type shell program which affords users quick and simple access to Internet services. You access the menu system from a direct terminal or with a modem and communications package from your personal computer. Then, to access gopher, you simply select it from the menu.
5. Last but certainly not least, users who work from the command prompt of a time-sharing system (such as UNIX or VMS) simply type **gopher** at the command prompt to begin using gopher.

If your university offers more than one of these options, you may want to try out several and see which connection you prefer.

This chapter will demonstrate ways to use gopher via several systems and also Veronica, the key-word search engine for gopher.

THE ROOT GOPHER

Once connected to your university time-sharing system via any gopher client software, you should be able to connect to the root gopher at your university. The word root is commonly used to describe the base level of a directory structure from which all other directories branch. Each gopher site has a root directory from which all the other directories in gopher space can be accessed. The root gopher menu for the University of Texas at El Paso is presented below:

```
              Internet Gopher Information Client v1.13
                  Root gopher server: gopher.utep.edu
   -->     1.  The University of Texas at El Paso.
           2.  UTEP Directory Services <?>
           3.  Graduate and Undergraduate Studies Catalog/
           4.  Geological Sciences/
           5.  College of Nursing and Health Sciences/
           6.  Urban Systemic Initiative (USI) Grant Reporting/
           7.  Software Distribution Library/
           8.  Rio Grande Free-Net <TEL>
           9.  All the Gopher Servers in the World/
          10.  GN Documentation/
```

Notice that the menu offers information about the university, a connection via Tel-net to a local freenet, and an option "All the Gopher Servers in the World." If you select the latter option, you can browse any number of gopher menus, looking for interesting stuff. Root gopher menus will vary in their content, but they generally offer both connections to items of interest only to that university or corporate community and connections to other gopher sites.

DIRECT GOPHER CONNECTION

You can also connect directly to a particular gopher if you know the address. For example, the address of the gopher in the first sample gopher session later in this chapter is **cwis.usc.edu,** so you could type **gopher cwis.usc.edu** at the UNIX command prompt (or whatever prompt is available through your software and connection type) and thus make a connection with the remote gopher.

GOPHER MENUS

Once you have established a connection with a remote gopher, follow the *menu trees** until you have found the information you are looking for. Gopher will

---

*Menu tree refers to the branching selections offered by a gopher. If you choose one option from the root gopher menu, for example, you receive a new menu of options related to that selection. You follow the branches of a menu tree until you reach the desired information.

often connect you to resources at other locations, hiding the computer boundaries completely so that the gopher server seems simply one large, menu-driven
system.

GOPHER PROVIDES ACCESS TO MORE
THAN TEXT DOCUMENTS

The type of information under each menu heading (text, picture, software,
etc.) can be determined by the item's gopher type ID. These IDs can be displayed on most mainframe systems; just select an item and type **=**. On most
PC clients you choose "Item Description" from the file menu. Macintosh
clients typically use command **i**. The following table lists ID types:

Type IDs and their meanings

0	Item is a file
1	Item is a directory
2	Item is a CSO phonebook server
3	Error (not compatible with gopher)
4	Item is a BinHexed Macintosh file
5	Item is DOS binary archive
6	Item is a UNIX unencoded file
7	Item is an index-search server
8	Item points to a text-based Telnet session
9	Item is a binary file. Client must read until the connection closes. Beware!
g	Item is a gift file
h	Item is html type
I	Item is an image type
i	Item is "inline" text type
M	Item is a MIME file
s	Item is a sound type
t	Item is a tn3270 connection

Fortunately, you should rarely have to worry about this information. Most advanced gopher clients can recognize these data types for you, and some even
provide you with a description rather than just the code.

Many gopher clients allow you to browse through a gopher menu by moving the arrow keys on your keyboard up or down. Selecting an item on the menu causes the next menu or file to be displayed. Other command options generally appear at the bottom of the menu. For example, with a UNIX gopher, the command options generally look like this:

```
Press ? for Help, q to Quit, u to go up a menu.
```

If you type the **?**, you will receive an extensive help menu with a listing of commands. While the individual commands will vary, these basic features are supported by all modern gopher clients. A more complete list of basic gopher commands is offered in the box below.

GOPHER COMMANDS

These are typical gopher commands. The commands on your gopher client may vary slightly.

Moving around:
Press return to view a document.
Use the arrow keys to move around.

Up	Move to previous line.
Down	Move to next line.
Right, Return	"Enter"/Display current item.
Left, u	"Exit" current item/Go up a level.
>, +, Pgdwn, space	View next page.
<, -, Pgup, b	View previous page.
0-9	Go to a specific line.
m	Go back to the main menu.

Bookmarks:
a: Add current item to the bookmark list.
A: Add current directory/search to bookmark list.
v: View bookmark list.
d: Delete a bookmark/directory entry.

Other Commands:
q: Quit with prompt.
Q: Quit unconditionally.
=: Display technical information about current item.
O: Change options.
/: Search for an item in the menu.
n: Find next search item.

Bookmarks

If you have a gopher on your university system (or in the case of PPP or SLIP, on your own computer), you can create your own custom gopher menu by placing bookmarks at gopher sites that interest you. The commands for this vary somewhat from system to system. The basic UNIX commands for bookmarks are listed in the box of gopher commands.

SAMPLE GOPHER SESSION VIA MENU-BASED SHELL SYSTEM

One of the most impressive clusters of archives accessible via gopher is called Gopher Jewels. Its home menu is located at the University of Southern California at the gopher address **cwis.usc.edu** (the numeric address is **128.125.253.146**). This gopher site is organized by subject and offers pointers or connections to other gophers with information on those subjects. In addition, it offers keyword search services for all of the gophers it indexes. Let's use it for a sample gopher session.

Begin by accessing your gopher client. The sample given here was created via the University of Texas at El Paso's menu-based system. When starting this gopher client, you are greeted with this screen:

```
Welcome to Gopher!  Symbolic tunneling through the INTERNET.
You may specify an IP address for the gopher hole of your choice.

A simple carriage return will GOPHER to Minnesota, (tradition.)

Other           1. utepvm.ep.utexas.edu          our own address(!)
suggestions:    2. dillon.geo.ep.utexas.edu      our Geology Dept.
                3. sjumusic.stjohns.edu          another MUSIC/SP

                4. tscc.macarthur.uws.edu.au yet another MUSIC/SP

                5. gopherhost.cc.utexas.edu      another UTEXAS site.
                6. bongo.cc.utexas.edu      still another UTEXAS site.
                7. marvel.loc.gov         Library of Congress server.
                8. iitf.doc.gov   National Info. Infrastructure

                9. gopher.utep.edu               another UTEP gopher.
We may add more later.
All will provide opportunity to switch around the network.
```

Notice that the screen offers the option of choosing one of the selected gophers listed or specifying the address of a specific gopher. This menu, while convenient, is not a gopher menu. It is simply a quick start list of bookmarks added by the local system administrators. Option 9 will take you to the root gopher shown previously, **gopher.utep.edu.** Many sites offering access to their services through a menu-based system, and a few of the basic UNIX or VMS sites, may add a similar kind of opening screen for the convenience of their users.

The UTEP opening screen invites you to "specify an IP address for the gopher hole of your choice." To connect to the University of Southern California gopher housing Gopher Jewels, type this address at the command line or prompt:

```
cwis.usc.edu.
```

Some gophers not using a menu-type system may require you to type the word **gopher** in front of the address:

```
gopher cwis.usc.edu.
```

Once your gopher client connects with the University of Southern California gopher, you receive the following screen:

```
Gopher Site: CWIS.USC.EDU (128.125.253.146) ---------
Command ==> _
enter selection  (8:Previous Menu or Exit, 0:Quit)
-----------------------------------------------------
    1 - About USCgopher <menu>
    2 - How To Find Things on Gopher <menu>
    3 - University Information <menu>
    4 - Campus Life <menu>
    5 - Computing Information <menu>
    6 - Library and Research Information <menu>
    7 - Health Sciences <menu>
    8 - Research and Technology Centers <menu>
    9 - Other Gophers and Information Resources <menu>
```

This is the root gopher menu for the University of Southern California. It offers some local information such as "Campus Life," and "University Information," as well as connections to other gophers and a number of Internet resources. Gopher Jewels can be reached by selecting option 9, "Other Gophers and Information Resources." This selection will take you to the following menu:

```
Gopher Site: cwis.usc.edu (128.125.253.146) -------------
Command ==> _
enter selection  (0:Previous Menu or Exit, Q:Quit)
-----------------------------------------------------------
     1 - How to use Gopher (free course) <menu>
     2 - Guides to Internet Resources <menu>
     3 - Gophers by Subject <menu>
     4 - Gophers by Location <menu>
     5 - Gophers by Keyword Search (Veronica) <menu>
     6 - The Mother Gopher at Minnesota <menu>
     7 - Internet File Server (FTP) Sites <menu>
     8 - Directories (names, phones, addresses) <menu>
     9 - Commercial Services <menu>
    10 - Clearinghouse for Subject-Oriented Internet Resource
    11 - Gopher-Jewels <menu>
    12 - Miscellaneous <menu>
    13 - Delphi Internet Services Holiday Gopher <menu>
```

Lots of interesting things here! You might want to look at some of them later, but for now select 11, "Gopher-Jewels." That selection results in this screen;

```
Gopher Site: cwis.usc.edu (128.125.253.146) -------------
Command ==> _
enter selection  (0:Previous Menu or Exit, Q:Quit)
-----------------------------------------------------------
     1 - GOPHER JEWELS Information and Help <menu>
     2 - Community, Global and Environmental <menu>
     3 - Education, Social Sciences, Arts & Humanities <menu>
     4 - Economics, Business and Store Fronts <menu>
     5 - Engineering and Industrial Applications <menu>
     6 - Government <menu>
     7 - Health, Medical, and Disability <menu>
     8 - Internet and Computer Related Resources <menu>
     9 - Law <menu>
    10 - Library, Reference, and News <menu>
    11 - Miscellaneous Items <menu>
    12 - Natural Sciences including Mathematics <menu>
    13 - Personal Development and Recreation <menu>
    14 - Research, Technology Transfer and Grants Opportunities <menu>
    15 - Search Gopher Jewels Menus by Key Word(s) <Index-Search>
```

A good place to start learning about Gopher Jewels might be option 1, "GO-PHER JEWELS Information and Help." Here is that menu:

```
Gopher Site: cwis.usc.edu (128.125.253.146) -------------
Command —>  _
enter selection  (0:Previous Menu or Exit, Q:Quit)
-----------------------------------------------------
   1 - About Gopher Jewels <text>
   2 - Select This Option To Leave Your Comments and Suggestions
   3 - What's New with Gopher Jewels <text>
   4 - Gopher Tips & Help Documents <menu>
   5 - Gopher Jewels Announcement Archives <menu>
   6 - Gopher Jewels Discussion   Archives <menu>
   7 - Gopher Jewels Mirror Sites Worldwide <menu>
   8 - Search Gopher Jewels Archives: Discussions, Announcements
   9 - Other Archives and Related Information <menu>
  10 -  Jump to Gopher Jewels Main Menu <menu>
  11 - Search Gopher Jewels Menus by Key Word(s) <Index-Search>
```

You can select option 1, "About Gopher Jewels," to receive a screen introducing Gopher Jewels, followed by pages of text. Below are the intro screen and the first page of text:

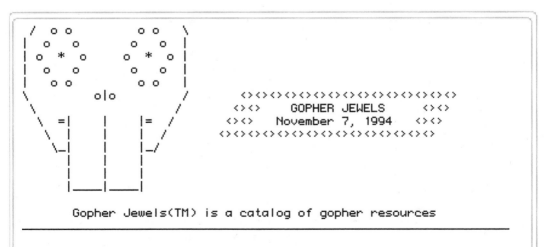

```
                              <><><><><><><><><><><><><><><>
                              <><>      GOPHER JEWELS      <><>
                              <><>    November 7, 1994     <><>
                              <><><><><><><><><><><><><><><>


         Gopher Jewels(TM) is a catalog of gopher resources
_____

  Gopher Jewels offers a unique approach to gopher subject tree
  design and content. It is an alternative to the more traditional
  subject tree design.  Although many of the features,
```

```
individually, are not new the combined set represents the best
features found on sites around the world.  We offer solutions to
navigating information by subject as an experiment in the
evolution of information cataloging. Our focus is on locating
information by subject and does not attempt to address the quality
of the information we point to.

Gopher Jewels offers the following:

- Over 2,000 pointers to information by category
- Jughead search of all menus in Gopher Jewels
- The option to jump up one menu level from any directory
- The option to jump to the top menu from any directory
- Gopher Tips help documents
- Gopher Jewels list archives
- Gopher Jewels - Talk list archives
- Other gopher related archives
- Help and archives searchable (WAIS)
```

Finally! This is an article explaining what Gopher Jewels is and how to use it. As you page through the explanation, notice that the list of subject categories includes environment, education, geography, economics, business, engineering, and law, just to list a few. There is also an explanation of how to use the keyword search through Gopher Jewels.

It might be useful to have a copy of this document. Move back to the previous menu. In the system used for this example, one would do so by pressing F3. In a UNIX system this command would be "u". Next select the file and issue a copy command (here F5; in UNIX, "D"). Most systems will prompt you for a filename and then will proceed to transfer the file to your account (or personal computer, depending on the restrictions of your system).

Now that you have completed your first transfer, you may want to spend a few minutes exploring. Gopher space is vast, so watch your time. It is easy to spend hours just window shopping.

SAMPLE GOPHER SESSION VIA TURBOGOPHER ON THE MACINTOSH

Network, SLIP, and PPP users have some even more powerful and easy-to-use gopher options. There are several pieces of gopher client software available for both PCs and Macs with this type of connection. One of the more commonly used packages is TurboGopher for the Macintosh. TurboGopher offers a friendly environment that resembles the Mac's own folder system of organization.

TurboGopher is built around the idea of multiple windows of file folders. When you first start TurboGopher, the standard default connection is made to the University of Minnesota (the site where the gopher protocol was developed). When the connection is made, the following window will appear:

```
┌─────────────────────────────────────────────────────────────────┐
│ ▣▣▣▣▣▣▣▣▣▣▣▣▣▣▣▣▣ Home Gopher Server ▣▣▣▣▣▣▣▣▣▣▣▣▣▣▣▣ ▣ │
├───────────────────────────────────────────────────────────────┤
│ ▼   Internet Gopher ©1991-1994 University of Minnesota.         │
├───────────────────────────────────────────────────────────────┤
│ 🗂📁 Information About Gopher                                 ⬆ │
│    📁 Computer Information                                       │
│ 🗂📁 Discussion Groups                                          │
│    📁 Fun & Games                                               │
│ 🗂📁 Internet file server (ftp) sites                           │
│ 🗂📁 Libraries                                                  │
│ 🗂📁 News                                                       │
│ 🗂📁 Other Gopher and Information Servers                       │
│ 🗂📁 Phone Books                                                │
│    ❓ Search Gopher Titles at the University of Minnesota       │
│    ❓ Search lots of places at the University of Minnesota      │
│ 🗂📁 University of Minnesota Campus Information               ⬇ │
├───────────────────────────────────────────────────────────────┤
│ ⬅ ▥▥▥▥▥▥▥▥▥▥▥▥▥▥▥▥▥▥▥▥▥▥▥▥▥▥▥▥▥▥▥▥▥▥▥▥▥▥▥▥▥ ➡ ▣ │
└─────────────────────────────────────────────────────────────────┘
```

Navigating through gopher menus with TurboGopher is easy. You simply double-click on a menu item to view it. The icons behave just like Macintosh folders, giving you the feeling that the Internet is simply an extension of your hard drive. But point-and-click access is not the only advantage of this type of software. TurboGopher also provides the most common gopher commands as menu options, saving you from having to remember what keystrokes and command sequences are required to submit a command to your client software. TurboGopher is also friendly with many other pieces of network software, allowing you to connect through Telnet or uncompress a document automatically, without the hassle of finding and loading other software manually.

Through TurboGopher you can quickly repeat the search for Gopher Jewels. You would begin by launching the TurboGopher application. Simply double-click on the TurboGopher icon. After a few moments, you will be connected to the default gopher menu at the University of Minnesota. Pull down the file menu and select the "Another Gopher . . ." command from the list. The following box will appear:

Connect to Another Gopher Server At:

Title:

Server name:

Server port: 70

Selector:

☐ Is a Gopher+ server

[Cancel]   [OK]

In the box for "Server name," type **cwis.usc.edu;** which is the address of the gopher server at the University of Southern California, where the Gopher Jewels archive is stored. Once you have typed in the server name, click on "OK" and you will receive the following gopher menu:

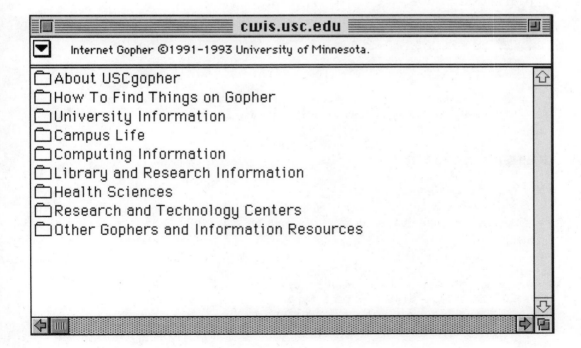

cwis.usc.edu

▼ Internet Gopher ©1991–1993 University of Minnesota.

📁 About USCgopher
📁 How To Find Things on Gopher
📁 University Information
📁 Campus Life
📁 Computing Information
📁 Library and Research Information
📁 Health Sciences
📁 Research and Technology Centers
📁 Other Gophers and Information Resources

From here you can follow the menu links, from "Other Gophers and Information Resources" to "Gopher Jewels," where you can explore the Gopher Jewels archive with a simple click of the mouse.

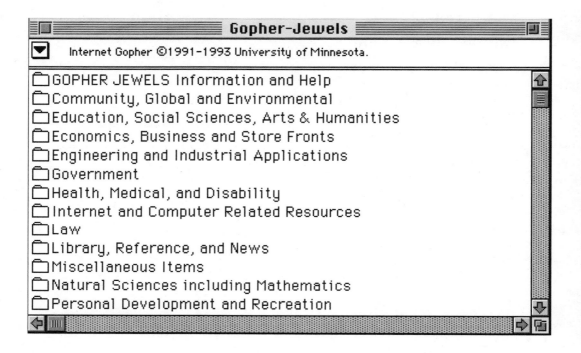

TurboGopher is one of dozens of network-based gopher clients. These are generally offered as shareware or freeware at many large FTP software archives.

GOPHER VIA TELNET

If your system does not have a gopher installed, you can telnet to one of many gophers. For example, you can telnet to **panda.uiowa.edu** for gopher access. The initial menu looks like this:

```
Welcome to Michigan State University
To use the public Gopher client type:          gopher
To use the public World-Wide Web client type:   web
To report problems, send mail to consult@msu.edu or call (517) 353-1800

          Internet Gopher Information Client v1.13
```

```
                        MSU Central Gopher

  -->   1.  Gopher at Michigan State University.
        2.  Help Using Gopher (More About Gopher)/
        3.  Keyword Search of Titles in MSU's Gopher <?>
        4.  About Michigan State University/
        5.  MSU Campus Events & Calendars/
        6.  News & Weather/
        7.  Phone Books & Other Directories/
        8.  Information for the MSU Community/
        9.  Computing & Technology/
       10.  Libraries/
       11.  MSU Services & Facilities/
       12.  Outreach / Extension / Community Affairs/
       13.  Network & Database Resources/

 Press ? for Help, q to Quit, u to go up a menu
```

As Internet traffic has increased in the last couple of years, a number of gopher sites making themselves available via Telnet have restricted use. Some of the gophers still offering Telnet connections at the time of this printing are the following:

NAME	LOG IN AS
consultant.micro.umn.edu	gopher
library.wustl.edu	(no log-in required)
panda.uiowa.edu	(no log-in required)
ux1.cso.uiuc.edu	gopher
gopher.msu.edu	gopher

HOW TO FIND GOPHERS

Gopher is one of the Internet's most powerful and user-friendly protocols. Knowing how to use it, however, is only part of the issue. You still have to find gophers containing information of interest to you. How do you do that? There are several methods:

1. Look at lists of gophers like the one in the next section or in books or on-line documents.
2. Explore major gopher sites such as Gopher Jewels to become familiar with their contents and the connections they offer to other gophers.
3. Use Veronica, the keyword search application for gopher (see later in this chapter), to generate a list of gophers that have texts on a particular topic.

4. Get to know your own site's gopher menus. They will often contain a surprising amount of information, saving you the trouble of searching through other sites in *gopherspace.**

SELECTED GOPHERS

To use the following addresses, access your gopher client and type the address. For example, from a UNIX gopher client you would need to type **gopher** before each of the addresses. For most of the gophers, a menu item of interest is listed; if you browse around in these gophers, you will also find other helpful information.

Agriculture (U.S. Department of Agriculture)
esusda.gov *or* **zeus.esusda.gov**
Biology
fragrans.riken.go.jp
life.anu.edu.au
Business Conferences
nysernet.org (/special collections, Business & Economic Development)
Careers (Online Career Center)
gopher.msen.com (/Msen Career Center)
Clearinghouse for Subject-Oriented Internet Resource Guides
una.hh.lib.umich.edu (/inetdirs)
Cyberspace
wiretap.spies.com
Economics
gopher.lib.umich.edu (/Social Sciences Resources/Economics)
niord.shsu.edu (/economics)
wuecon.wustl.edu
Education (U.S. Deptartment of Education)
gopher.ed.gov
English
english-server.hss.cmu.edu
Environment (Environmental Protection Agency)
futures.wic.epa.gov
Federal Documents
wiretap.spies.com

*Gopherspace is the worldwide system of gophers which are seamlessly interconnected via the Internet. Beginning at any gopher, one can access information at any other gopher.

Federal Information Exchange

> **fedix.fie.com**
>
> Information on research programs, grants, fellowships, minority programs.

Freenets

> **marvel.loc.gov** (/Internet Resources/Freenet Systems)

Geology (U.S. Geological Survey)

> **info.er.usgs.gov**

Gopher Jewels

> **cwis.usc.edu** (/Other Gophers and Information Resources/
> Gopher by Subject/ Gopher Jewels)

Health (National Institute of Health, including CancerNet, National AIDS Information Clearinghouse)

> **gopher.nih.gov**

Internet Documents

> **una.hh.lib.umich.edu** (/inetdirs)

Law

> **gopher.LAW.csuohio.edu**
>
> **fatty.LAW.cornell.edu**

Library of Congress Information System (LOCIS)

> **marvel.loc.gov** (/Library of Congress Online Information Systems)

Math

> **archives.math.utk.edu**

NASA

> **gopher.gsfc.nasa.gov**
>
> Information on shuttle launches, the environment, weather.

Philosophy (American Philosophy Association)

> **apa.oxy.edu**

Psychology

> **gopher.uottawa.ca**

Science (National Science Foundation)

> **stis.nsf.gov** (log in as public)
>
> Research publications and connections to other government sites.

Stock Market

> **lobo.rmhs.colorado.edu** (/other information sources)

White House Press Releases and Position Papers

> **marvel.loc.gov** (/Federal Government Information/Federal
> Information Resources/ Information by Agency/Executive Branch/White
> House)

CAMPUS WIDE INFORMATION SYSTEMS

Suppose you want to know your university's basketball schedule for next spring. You could call the athletic office. Or, if you are connected to the university's network, you can consult the Campus Wide Information System (CWIS). If you are thinking of transferring to Colorado College or New York University (or any other major college or university), you could write for information. Or, if you use the gopher connection, you can consult the CWIS for that school. CWISs provide a wide range of information, including course catalogs, campus facts, sports and other activity schedules, and job openings.

You can reach your university's CWIS through a menu option, or the university's gopher, or other location (if you don't find it easily, ask your help desk personnel).

To explore other universities' CWISs, gopher to **gopher.msu.edu** (Michigan State University). Or FTP a list of CWISs at **sunsite.unc.edu** (Directory: **pub/docs/about-the-net/cwis/cwis-l** [the last directory ends in the letter l]).

GOPHER IS GREAT! WHY USE ANYTHING ELSE?

Gopher is very powerful and provides vast access to many types of resources. However, it does have its limitations. Much of the activity once supported by gopher has recently moved to the World Wide Web. With the change in user preference has come a slowing of the construction of new menus for gopher. While this fact certainly does not mean gopher is an outdated or useless protocol, it does mean that the newest resources on the Internet may take longer to appear in gopher menus then in the past. At least for the present, however, gopher remains one of the most powerful and useful tools available to the modern student.

VERONICA

Veronica (Very Easy Rodent-Oriented Net-wide Index to Computerized Archives) is a keyword search system which was developed to ease the process of finding information via gopher. It is provided at several server sites around the world. A Veronica server system maintains an index of gopher menu items. The Veronica program queries gopher servers biweekly and saves the information it collects in a giant database. When you submit a search to Veronica, it searches its database and sends your gopher client a customized gopher menu, which can be used in the same manner as any other gopher menu.

Using Veronica, for example, one could search for gophers that house information about tulips or baseball or any other topic. Many major gopher sites, through their menu options, offer a connection to a Veronica system. The option usually reads something like "Search Topics in Gopherspace Using Veronica." If you select this option from the University of Southern California gopher, which houses Gopher Jewels, **cwis.usc.edu,** you will get a menu like this:

```
Gophers by Keyword Search (Veronica)

 -->  1. How to Compose Veronica Queries - June 23, 1994
      2. Frequently-Asked Questions (FAQ) about Veronica - January 13, 1995
      3. More Veronica: Software, Index-Control Protocol, HTML homepage/

         Simplified Veronica chooses server - pick a search type:
      6. Simplified Veronica: Find Gopher MENUS only <?>
      7. Simplified Veronica: find ALL gopher types <?>

      9. Find GOPHER DIRECTORIES by Title word(s) (via NYSERNet) <?>
     10. Find GOPHER DIRECTORIES by Title word(s) (via UNINETT..of Bergen)
     11. Find GOPHER DIRECTORIES by Title word(s) (via PSINet) <?>
     12. Find GOPHER DIRECTORIES by Title word(s) (via SUNET) <?>
     13. Find GOPHER DIRECTORIES by Title word(s) (via U. of Manitoba) <?>
     14. Search GopherSpace by Title word(s) (via NYSERNet) <?>
     15. Search GopherSpace by Title word(s) (via UNINETT/U. of Bergen) <?>
     16. Search GopherSpace by Title word(s) (via PSINet) <?>
     17. Search GopherSpace by Title word(s) (via SUNET) <?>
     18. Search GopherSpace by Title word(s) (via U. of Manitoba) <?>

Press ? for Help, q to Quit, u to go up a menu
```

Some of these Veronica sites are in the United States and some in Europe. Occasionally a list will even include sites in Africa and Australia. Internet courtesy dictates that you use the ones closest to you in order to cut down on transmission distance, so try the ones near you first.

As you look through this Veronica menu, notice that two different search types are offered: "all titles," and "directory titles." The first means that Veronica will search through all information stored for each gopher, including the files themselves. The second option means that only the directories or menus are searched, not the files. Logically, the first type will result in more "hits" or a longer list of potential gopher sources, and the second type of search will be faster.

HOW DO YOU USE VERONICA?

Begin by connecting to your gopher client. There are many gateways to Veronica from gopher sites the world over. If you have trouble locating one, there is a Veronica listing in the University of Southern California gopher mentioned earlier, **cwis.usc.edu.** Different versions of the Veronica software are used at different sites. Some versions allow the use of multiple words, while others allow only a single keyword.

Choose one of the Veronica sites from the menu. The gopher client will respond with a box allowing you to submit the word or words for your search. The following is a typical Veronica search dialogue:

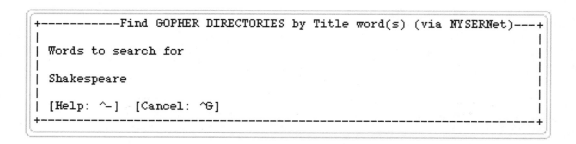

```
+-----------Find GOPHER DIRECTORIES by Title word(s) (via NYSERNet)---+
|                                                                     |
| Words to search for                                                 |
|                                                                     |
| Shakespeare                                                         |
|                                                                     |
| [Help: ^-]  [Cancel: ^G]                                            |
+---------------------------------------------------------------------+
```

A single word search might return just a few options or might return hundreds. For example, **Shakespeare** might return dozens of options. More concise searches are possible with the use of Boolean operator* words such as *and, or,* and *not* that are used to limit a search. For example, a search for **Shakespeare and Hamlet** will produce a different set of items than a search for **Shakespeare** because it will return only options that include both the word *Shakespeare* and the word *Hamlet.* **Shakespeare or Hamlet** will return a menu listing items containing either the word *Shakespeare* or the word *Hamlet.* **Shakespeare not Hamlet** will return a list of Shakespeare headings that do not contain the word *Hamlet.*

Another special option allows you to submit word strings for a search by enclosing the words in double quotes. For example, "**Early Shakespeare Drama**" will search for items containing those three words, connected, in that order (e.g., Early Shakespeare Drama, not Early Dramas by Shakespeare).

Some Veronica servers also allow you to use an asterisk (*) as a wild card. For example you can submit **Shakes*** and you will get a menu consisting of words beginning with the letters *Shakes* and ending with anything (e.g., Shakespeare, Shakespearean, Shakes and Malts, Earthquake shakes up Japan).

---

*Boolean operators or logical operators are words that specify the logical relationships between two concepts.

Be aware that there are few Veronica servers and much demand for their services. When you try to use Veronica, you may find that the connection is busy or does not respond. Try other Veronica servers on the menu list, and hopefully you will find one that responds.

JUGHEAD

Another type of index search found as a menu item on many major gopher sites is Jughead (Junzy's Universal Gopher Hierarchy Excavation and Display). It is used for searching within a particular gopher hierarchy and is very useful for major gopher sites such as Gopher Jewels.

ASSIGNMENTS

1. Connect to the home gopher at your university. Explore the menu branches, noting what information is given about your university and what links are provided for connecting to other gophers. Write a memo about what you find.
2. Connect to several of the gophers in the list provided in this chapter. Explore their menus and texts. Discuss what you find with other students in a small group. Write a memo about one of the gophers and the information it offers.
3. Consult other books about the Internet and locate three gophers in a subject area that interests you. Connect to those gophers and explore the information that they make available. Report what you find to the class in either an oral report or a memo.
4. Using Veronica, explore gophers that have texts related to your major. Create a custom gopher guide for those in your major, explaining how to use gopher and including a list of gophers with pertinent information.
5. After you have explored several gophers, write a report evaluating gopher as an Internet navigation tool. Indicate whether you found gopher easy or difficult to learn and whether you think you could find useful information by using gopher.

QUESTIONS TO ASK

1. Try accessing gopher using the methods listed on page 97. If they don't work, ask your instructor or system's administrator how to access gopher at your university.
2. What are the commands used for moving around in gopherspace (i.e., do you use "u" for up a menu or F3 or whatever)?
3. How do you download information from gopher? Can you copy directly to the hard disk of the computer you are using? If you need to copy to your ac-

count in the university's system, how do you do that and how do you then download it to a computer connected to the system?

4. If your university has a menu-driven system, does it have a list of interesting gophers already accessible on it?

5. Do you have a bookmark option on your university's gopher? (Bookmarks allow you to create a custom gopher menu with direct connections to gophers you find of interest.) If so, how does it work?

6. Does your university have a local Veronica client? If so, what commands are available when you use it?

NINE

FILE TRANSFER PROTOCOL (FTP)

FTP stands for File Transfer Protocol. It is the protocol which was designed specifically to transfer files between computers on the Internet. Like gopher, FTP is a client/server program, which means that when you use FTP you access client software that, with a few commands, establishes a connection with a remote computer that is running server software. This connection allows you to explore the remote computer's directories and download files. When you use FTP, the Internet resembles a huge disk drive attached to your computer.

FTP was developed in the 1970s by ARPAnet users and has been a popular protocol ever since. While not very user friendly, FTP has the advantage of being very portable; that is, it is able to run on many different types of computers.

There are two kinds of FTP: full-service FTP and anonymous FTP. Full-service FTP allows you to transfer files between any two computers on the Internet for which you have passwords or access privileges. Anonymous FTP allows anyone to retrieve publicly available files from several thousand different computers on the Internet. What kind of files? All kinds. How many? Millions! Some are computer programs that the authors allow to be copied freely and used with little or no fee. Other files available at these sites include thousands of digital images from both professional and amateur artists, digitized sound recordings ranging from industrial rock to Mozart, and hundreds of thousands of text documents covering a tremendous range of topics. Anonymous FTP is a privilege granted to users on the Internet by the administrators of sites containing these archives. What we will be primarily concerned with are the libraries of documents available by anonymous FTP that can be a valuable research aid to any student. These documents explore areas ranging from the North American Free Trade Agreement to the National Center for

Biotechnology and from new ideas for the social sciences to Project Gutenberg's text for "Peter Pan."

FTP may be the easiest protocol to use when you know where a file is located. Although many Internet sites are now offering access to their archives through gopher and World Wide Web, some important files are still available only through FTP. It is an older protocol, however, and doesn't have the user-friendly menu access of gopher and WWW; therefore, it presents certain difficulties when you are looking for information and don't know exactly where it is located. This chapter will first explain some easy ways to use FTP and then describe the less user-friendly UNIX access. It will also demonstrate Archie, a protocol for searching FTP sites by keyword, which solves many of the problems associated with FTP.

HOW DO YOU USE FTP?

Begin by accessing an FTP program (called an FTP client). Many different FTP programs are available, but most work in basically the same way. Universities offer access to FTP via a terminal connected to a time-sharing system such as UNIX, VAX/VMS, or IBM/VM. They may also offer FTP access through your home computer with the use of a modem. You log into your account on a time-sharing system, use that system to transfer files to your account, and then transfer files from your time-sharing account to your home computer with another communications program. More advanced connections which utilize graphical-style interfaces offer point-and-click FTP clients, such as WinFTP, Fetch, and X-FerIt, which are frequently available in university computer labs. If your system supports SLIP or PPP connections, you can install and operate one of these more advanced connections on your own computer. You will need to find out how to access an FTP client at your university. The process will probably be similar but not identical to one of the sample FTP sessions described in this chapter.

One of the easiest ways to use FTP, however, is not through an FTP client at all but through gopher. If you have studied the gopher chapter, you are already familiar with the powerful menu access it offers. You can put this same menu structure to work on FTP sites, organizing their directories into menus. Also, you can view text using FTP via gopher, something not possible (or at least not easy) with many FTP clients. FTP access is also available through WWW (see Chapter 7), but gopher access is still much more extensive because WWW is a much younger protocol. Some FTP sites still are not properly configured for WWW access.

Following are three sample FTP sessions, two easy approaches and one not so easy.

EASY FTP OPTION 1: GOPHER FTP

Suppose you want to use FTP to obtain a list of free books now available from Project Gutenberg. The project is named after Johann Gutenberg, a fifteenth-century German who is credited with being the first European to print with movable type, thus changing forever the way books are published. Project Gutenberg, directed by Michael Hart, is trying to revolutionize the publishing process once again. The goal is, by the year 2001, to have copied the texts of 10,000 books into a form accessible on the Internet and to provide these texts free of charge. Hart and his volunteers have been at this for some 25 years and have made quite a bit of progress.

Does it sound interesting to be able to download any of hundreds of the best books ever written? The index of books is available by FTP from a site with the address **mrcnext.cso.uiuc.edu.** Like gopher and WWW sites, FTP sites have unique addresses which allow you to point your FTP client to a particular machine on the Internet. If you know the address of the Project Gutenberg site, you have all the information you need to access and download the index.

To establish a connection with the FTP site for Project Gutenberg, first access your university's gopher client (see Chapter 8), then contact a major gopher server site that offers FTP connections (if your university system offers this itself, you save a step). For example, connect to the gopher at the University of Urbana-Champaign by typing the following:

```
gopher.uiuc.edu
```

You will receive this screen:

```
Gopher Site: GOPHER.UIUC.EDU (128.174.5.49)---------Line 1 OF 14
Command ==>                            BookMark ==> <none>
Enter selection (0:Previous Menu or Exit. Q:Quit Menu Depth: 1
----------------------------------------------------------------
1 - Welcome to the University of Illinois at Urbana-Champaign Gopher
2 - Campus Announcements (last updated 1/06/94) <menu>
3 - What's New? (last update: 3/15/94) <menu>
4 - Information about Gopher <menu>
5 - Keyword Search of UIUC Gopher Menus <Index-Search>
6 - Univ. of illinois at Urbana-Champaign Campus Information <menu>
7 - Champaign-Urbana & Regional Information <menu>
8 - Computer Documentation, Software, and Information <menu>
9 - Libraries and Reference Information <menu>
10 - Publications (U of I Press, Newspapers, Newsletters, etc.) & Weather <menu>
11 - Other Gopher and Information Servers <menu>
12 - Phone Books (ph) <menu>
13 - Internet File Server (ftp) Sites <menu>
14 - Disability Information and Resources <menu>
```

Select option 13, "Internet File Server (FTP) Sites." This screen appears:

```
Gopher Site: GOPHER.UIUC.EDU (128.174.5.49)---------Line 1 OF 36
Command ==>                                    BookMark ==> <none>
Enter selection (0:Previous Menu or Exit. Q:Quit Menu Depth: 2
-------------------------------------------------------------------
 1 - About this directory <text>
 2 - About Anonymous FTP <text>
 3 - Search of Most FTP sites (archie) <Index-Search>
 4 - Keyword Search of Entries in FTP Menus <Index-Search>
 5 - FTP.CSO: University of Illinois CCSO's Main FTP Server <menu>
 6 - FTP.NCSA: University of Illinois NCSA's Main FTP Server <menu>
 7 - Boombox at Minnesota, Home of the Gopher and POPmail <menu>
 8 - Type in the ftp site name for direct access <Index-Search>
 9 - Wuarchive.wustl.edu 128.252.135.4 GNU. X.11R3, GIF, IEN. RFSs, <menu>
10 - Popular FTP Sites via Gopher <menu>
11 - FTP sites that start with `a' <menu>
12 - b <menu>
13 - c <menu>
14 - d <menu>
15 - e <menu>
16 - f <menu>
17 - g <menu>
18 - h <menu>
```

You are looking for option 8, "Type in the ftp site name for direct access." When you select option 8, you receive this screen:

```
Gopher Site: GOPHER.UIUC.EDU (128.174.5.49)--------------------
Command ==>
Type in your search string and press Enter

-------------------------------------------------------------

-------------------------------------------------------------

                          Indexed Search Query

Instructions:Type in your search keywords below, separated by blanks, and press
Enter to start your search, or press F3 to exit.

Keywords ==>

Time to Wait ==> 40 (seconds) - when this time is up, quit searching
-------------------------------------------------------------
```

Wait a moment. This asks for keywords. What does that mean? This particular gopher client is using the same screen it uses for an Archie keyword search (which will be discussed later in this chapter). Ignore the request for keywords and type the address of the FTP site. Some gopher clients ask for an address and others leave a blank. Type the address **mrcnext.cso.uiuc.edu,** and the gopher connects you to the FTP archive sites housing Project Gutenberg. You receive the site's first FTP directory arranged by gopher as a menu.

```
Gopher Site: GOPHER.UIUC.EDU (128.174.5.49)---------Line 1 OF 21
Command ==>                               BookMark ==> <none>
Enter selection (O:Previous Menu or Exit. Q:Quit Menu Depth: 3
------------------------------------------------------------
1 - README <text>
2 - amiga <menu>
3 - asre <menu>
4 - bin <menu>
5 - compucon <menu>
6 - cycle <menu>
7 - etc <menu>
8 - etext <menu>
9 - gutenberg <menu>
10 - gutenberg.doc <text>
11 - kites <menu>
12 - lists <menu>
13 - local <menu>
14 - ls-1R.Z <binary>
15 - mac <menu>
16 - nethack <menu>
17 - pub <menu>
18 - uiuc <menu>
```

Item 1 is a README file. Whenever you see one of those at an FTP site, it is a good idea to read it because README files generally give an overview of the contents of the site archive. Select item 1 by typing the number 1 at the command prompt (or by highlighting item 1), touch <ENTER>, and receive this screen:

```
@GOPHERFILE                                    Rec 1/53
Command ==>                                    Scroll ==> PAGE
*** Top of file***-----------------------------VC/TEXTLC/IGNORE

Welcome to MRCNeXT, an '040 NeXT cube with 24mb ram and about 5 gigs
online. This machine lives in the CCSO - Micro Resource Center in 1420
DCL. Anonymous ftp access is granted 24 hours.

Files/directories of interest:

/pub/etext
                    The home site for Michael Hart's Project
                    Gutenberg electronic text collection. (Our
                    most popular item.)
```

```
/pub/linus
                        A  complete  mirror  archive  of  linus  from
                        sunsite.unc.edu and ftp.cdrom.com. (mirored
                        nightly)

/pub/info-mac
                        A  mirror  of  the  info-mac  archive  from
                        sumex-aim.stanford.edu. (mirrored nightly)
```

This first page of the README file explains that the Project Gutenberg collection is in directory **/pub/etext.** Exit this screen with an F3 (your exit command may be different). Looking again at the previous gopher screen you will see a listing for the pub directory, item 17. Select it and this screen appears:

```
Gopher Site: GOPHER.UIUC.EDU (128.174.5.49)---------Line 1 OF 15
Command ==>                                      BookMark ==> <none>
Enter selection (O:Previous Menu or Exit. Q:Quit Menu Depth: 4
-----------------------------------------------------------------
1 - doom <menu>
2 - etext <menu>
3 - gnu <menu>
4 - info-mac <menu>
5 - jgross <menu>
6 - jwessel <menu>
7 - linux <menu>
8 - mac <menu>
9 - mirror <menu>
10 - pc <menu>
11 - pcsig <menu>
12 - sounds <menu>
13 - unix <menu>
14 - win3 <menu>
15 - zsh <menu>
```

The etext directory is item 2. Select it and receive this screen:

```
Gopher Site: GOPHER.UIUC.EDU (128.174.5.49)---------Line 1 OF 20
Command ==>                                      BookMark ==> <none>
Enter selection (O:Previous Menu or Exit. Q:Quit Menu DeptÍÍÍh: 5
-----------------------------------------------------------------
1 - .dir3_O.wmd <text>
2 - .hidden <text>
```

```
 3 - OIndex.GUT <text>
 4 - INDEX.100.GUT <text>
 5 - INDEX.200.GUT <text>
 6 - INDEX.400.GUT <text>
 7 - LIST.COM <text>
 8 - NEWUSER.GUT <text>
 9 - articles <menu>
10 - etext90 <menu>
11 - etext 91 <menu>
12 - etext 92 <menu>
13 - etext 93 <menu>
14 - etext 94 <menu>
15 - etext 95 <menu>
16 - freenet <menu>
17 - hart <menu>
18 - ippe <menu>
```

Wait. There are several items labeled index. You can tell that they are documents because of the <text> extensions after the file names. You do not know which is the main index. If you take a guess and request the one listed first, item 3 "0INDEX.GUT," this is the first screen of the index you will see:

```
Gopher Site: GOPHER.UIUC.EDU (128.174.5.49)-------Line 1 OF 486
Command ==>                              Scroll ==> PAGE
*** Top of file ***_____VC/TEXTIC/IGNORE

etext94:
total 106337

-rwxr-xr-x 1 hart                593683 Sep 2 12:07 2000010.txt
-rwxr-xr-x 1 hart                246689 Sep 2 12:08 2000010.zip
-rwxr-xr-x 1 hart                787707 Jun 20 1994 2city11.txt
-rwxr-xr-x 1 hart                325782 Jun 20 1994 2city11.zip
-rwxr-xr-x 1 hart               5262079 May 1 1994 2sqrt10a.txt
-rwxr-xr-x 1 hart               2624036 May 2 1994 2sqrt10a.zip
-rwxr-xr-x 1 hart                160780 Jan 2 1994 80day10.txt
-rwxr-xr-x 1 hart                160780 Jan 2 1994 80day10.zip
-rwxr-xr-x 1 hart                  9188 Dec 12 16:39 INDEX100.GUT
-rwxr-xr-x 1 hart                  7086 Dec 12 16:29 INDEX200.GUT
-rwxr-xr-x 1 hart                   703 Dec 12 16:27 INDEX400.GUT
-rwxr-xr-x 1 hart                748407 Aug 15 17:33 algif10.zip
-rwxr-xr-x 1 hart                267804 Sep 20 08:17 amdag10.txt
-rwxr-xr-x 1 hart                104230 Sep 22 04:37 amdag10.zip
-rwxr-xr-x 1 hart                181384 Sep 12 04:18 amdgf10.zip
-rwxr-xr-x 1 hart                770917 Sep 1 03:02 ameri10.txt
-rwxr-xr-x 1 hart                316909 Sep 1 03:03 ameri10.zip
```

This isn't very helpful. There are lots of files listed but no explanation. This is not an uncommon experience in an FTP site; often you must do a little exploring to find the path to the document you want. Exit this document and try option 4, the second index listed, "INDEX100.GUT." Finally you have found an index!

```
@GOPHERFILE                                  Rec 1/164
Command ==>                                  Scroll ==> PAGE
*** Top of file***-----------------------------VC/TEXTLC/IGNORE
This is an index of the first 100 Project Gutenberg Etexts [gutindex.100] mh

[Pre-1991 etexts are now in > cd/etext/etext90.
[These 199x etexts are now in > cd/etext/etext9x]
[Do a dir *.zip or dir *.text to see exact names.]

[Short index is updated every day. get 0INDEX.GUT from /etext/articles]

Mon Year                 Title/Author                 [filename.ext] ##

Jan  1994   The Complete Works of William Shakespeare [LOF] shaks10x.xxx 100C
Jan  1994   Ludwig van Beethoven, 5th Symphony in c-minor #67 [1vb5s10x.xxx] 99
Jan  1994   A Tale of Two Cities, by Charles Dickens [CD#1] [2city10x.xxx] 98
Jan  1994   Flatland, by Edwin A. Abbott [Math in Fiction] [flat10xx.xxx] 97
Jan  1994   The Monster Men, by Edgar Rice Burroughs [monst10x.xxx] 96

Dec  1993   The Prisoner of Zenda, by Anthony Hope [zenda10x.xxx] 95
```

The document says that it is an index for the first 100 etexts produced by Project Gutenberg. There is even an explanation for the content of the 0INDEX.GUT file (the one you tried first, remember?); it is a short index updated every day. Now that you have an index, you might like to know how to download the books prepared by the project. Exit the document and look again at the last menu. Likely there are instructions stored in one of the options. There is an option 9 called "articles." That sounds like it may offer some information about the Gutenberg project. Select it and receive another menu (only the second screen of the text is displayed below).

```
Gopher Site: GOPHER.UIUC.EDU (128.174.5.49)--------Line 19 OF 27
Command ==>                                  BookMark ==> <none>
Enter selection (0:Previous Menu or Exit. Q:Quit Menu Depth: 6
-------------------------------------------------------------

19 - nren.txt <text>
20 - o640.gif <binary>
```

```
21 - progress <text>
22 - savenet.994 <text>
23 - standard.494 <text>
24 - standard.d93 <text>
25 - standard.gut <text>
26 - suggest.gut <text>
27 - www.$ <text>
```

If you try several of the options on this menu, you will find the information under option 26, "suggest.gut." This document explains how to obtain Project Gutenberg texts by FTP and electronic mail. Here is the part of the file with those instructions:

```
@GOPHERFILE                                    Rec 39/137
Command ==>                                     Scroll ==> PAGE
*** Top of file***-----------------------------VC/TEXTLC/IGNORE

To retrieve a file via ftp:

ftp oes.orst.edu (129.193.124.1)
Log in as `anonymous' and your login name as a password.
cd/pub/almanac/etext or cd/pub/almanac/guten (dir/ls to check)
ls          (to get a list of files)
bin         (to switch to binary mode)
get filename (where `filename' was one of the files listed)
bye         (when done)

To retrieve a file via e-mail, first send the following line by itself to
almanac@oes.orst.edu

     send gutenberg catalog

This will instruct you how to send further requests, and will list the available
files. For example, to retrieve _Alice's Adventures in Wonderland_, send to
almanac@oes.orst.edu
     send gutenberg alice
```

Congratulations! If you have used gopher FTP to retrieve your own index from Project Gutenberg, you have completed your first FTP session! You have some potentially useful information from an FTP archive and have the necessary knowledge to explore any of the thousands of other FTP archives.

EASY FTP OPTION 2: FETCH FOR MACINTOSH

Fetch is a Macintosh program for transferring files via FTP. It is intended for use on any Macintosh computer connected to the Internet either by network link, SLIP, or PPP. Fetch provides quick point-and-click access to any FTP site, thus reducing the difficuly of browsing through directories with cryptic commands and providing FTP with a structure as simple as opening a file on your computer.

When you start Fetch, the Fetch main window will be displayed on your screen along with the connection dialogue box.

```
╔═══════════ Open Connection... ═══════════╗
║                                           ║
║  Enter host name, user name, and password ║  ction...  ⌘O
║  (or choose from the shortcut menu):      ║
║                                           ║  Status
║  Host:      [                        ]    ║    Not connected.
║                                           ║
║  User ID:   [                        ]    ║  File
║                                           ║
║  Password:  [                        ]    ║
║                                           ║
║  Directory: [                        ]    ║  Transfer
║                                           ║
║  Shortcuts: [▼]   ( Cancel )  (( OK ))    ║
║                                           ║
╚═══════════════════════════════════════════╝  2.1.2
```

To begin your session, fill in the blanks in the box. First specify the name or IP address of the host to which you wish to connect. For this example we will use **mrcnext.cso.uiuc.edu,** the address of the anonymous FTP host at the University of Iowa at Urbana-Champaign where the files of Project Gutenberg are stored. As in the previous gopher FTP example, we will be looking for an index listing Project Gutenberg's electronic texts. Next you may enter a user ID and password. If you do not enter a user ID, Fetch will use the default of "anonymous." Most of the time, including this example, you will be using Fetch for anonymous FTP, so you will rarely need to fill in this line. It is courteous to include your e-mail address as your password for anonymous FTP. While it is not always necessary to do so, some hosts will not allow access without it, so you should make a habit of filling in this blank (after exploring the features of Fetch, you will find that you can choose to have Fetch fill in this line for you). The last line in the box allows you to specify the name of the directory within the remote site where you wish to begin. This line is useful if you are familiar with a host and know which directory to select. For now you should leave this line blank, thereby telling Fetch to default to the host's root directory.

Once you have filled in the dialogue box, you are ready to go. Press the "OK" button at the bottom of the box, and Fetch will automatically establish the connection. Next Fetch will take a moment to list the directory specified in the connection dialogue box. Since you left that item blank, Fetch will default to the local root directory. Fetch displays directories in roughly the same way that the Macintosh system displays folders. Once you are connected, the current remote directory is displayed in a pop-up menu above the file list. The root directory is usually represented by a / (divide sign).

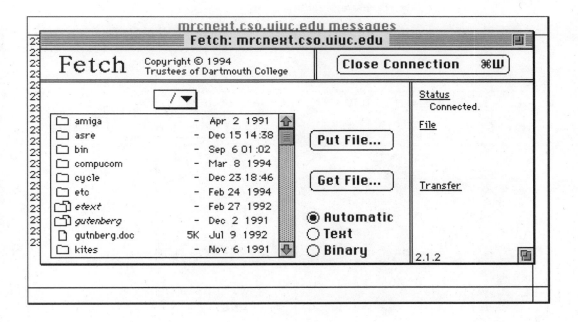

You are now connected to the root directory at this FTP host. The window that just appeared behind the main window is the host message window. You can click on that window to bring it to the surface. This window displays any messages that the remote host sends to you. These include messages about proper system usage and the current usage statistics at the site. This site has also included a note that the files for Project Gutenberg can be found in the directory **/pub/etext.** Now that you have seen the messages window, move back to the main Fetch window by clicking on it, and we will continue.

The main window is broken up into several sections. The left side is dominated by the file list, a scrollable list that shows the names of all of the files and directories contained within the current working directory. Because the host message told us the location of the Project Gutenberg files, we should begin by changing the current working directory from the root to **/pub/etext.**

Fetch allows you to change directories in several ways. Double-clicking on a directory name in the file list will move you to that directory. Selecting the "Change Directory . . ." command from the Directories menu will bring up a dialogue box requesting the path name of the directory that you wish to enter. Third, the pop-up menu above the file list (containing the name of the current directory) will allow you to move to any of the directories that lie between the current directory and the root.

By simply clicking on "pub" in the file list, you change the working directory from the root to "pub." Next, in that file list, clicking on "etext" will change the working directory to **/pub/etext** (note that the pop-up menu above the file list now reads "etext"). You are now in the directory containing the files pertaining to Project Gutenberg. Take a moment to examine the file list.

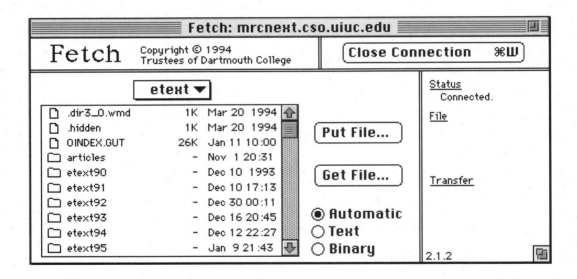

It would be wise to take this opportunity to check for system notices containing special information relevant to this directory. These are usually contained in files entitled "README" or "Index." They will contain messages about the location, size, and purpose of different files within the directory. The first one we find is named "0index.gut." In order to view this file, highlight "0index.gut" in the file list and then select the "View File . . ." command from the Remote menu in the menu bar (see below).

This will open a new window, and the text for "0index.gut" will begin to appear.

```
                                  OINDEX.GUT
etext94:
total 106337
-rwxr-xr-x  1 hart        593683 Sep  2 12:07 2000010.txt
-rwxr-xr-x  1 hart        246689 Sep  2 12:08 2000010.zip
-rwxr-xr-x  1 hart        787707 Jun 20  1994 2city11.txt
-rwxr-xr-x  1 hart        325782 Jun 20  1994 2city11.zip
-rwxr-xr-x  1 hart       5262079 May  1  1994 2sqrt10a.txt
-rwxr-xr-x  1 hart       2624036 May  2  1994 2sqrt10a.zip
-rwxr-xr-x  1 hart        385824 Jan  2  1994 80day10.txt
-rwxr-xr-x  1 hart        160780 Jan  2  1994 80day10.zip
-rwxr-xr-x  1 hart          9188 Dec 12 16:39 INDEX100.GUT
-rwxr-xr-x  1 hart          7086 Dec 12 16:27 INDEX200.GUT
-rw-r--r--  1 hart           703 Dec 12 16:27 INDEX400.GUT
-rwxr-xr-x  1 hart        748407 Aug 15 17:33 algif10.zip
-rwxr-xr-x  1 hart        267804 Sep 20 08:17 amdag10.txt
-rwxr-xr-x  1 hart        104230 Sep 22 04:37 amdag10.zip
-rwxr-xr-x  1 hart        181384 Sep 12 04:18 amdgf10.zip
-rwxr-xr-x  1 hart        770917 Sep  1 03:02 ameri10.txt
-rwxr-xr-x  1 hart        316909 Sep  1 03:03 ameri10.zip
-rw-r--r--  1 hart        863519 Nov 26 12:28 apoc10.txt
-rw-r--r--  1 hart        316147 Nov 26 12:29 apoc10.zip
-rwxr-xr-x  1 hart        863519 Mar 31  1994 apoc9.txt
```

This does not look very helpful. There is a lot of information listed but no explanation. Perhaps another index would be more helpful. Close this window and return to the main window.

Scrolling through the file list, you see that the next index in the list is "index 100.gut." Select this file and use the "View File . . ." command again to take a look at this index.

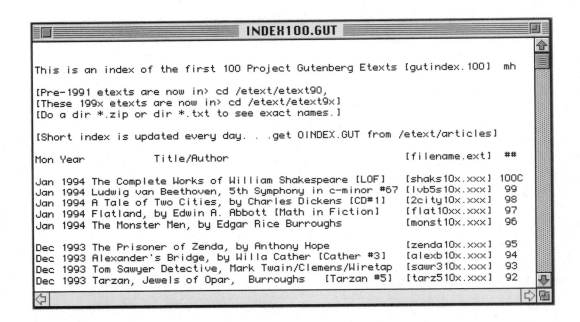

Finally, something that makes sense! The document says that it is an index for the first 100 etexts produced by Project Gutenberg. There is even an explanation for the content of the "0index.gut" file: It is a short index updated every day. Now that you have an index, you might like to know how to download books prepared by the project.

Begin by returning to the Fetch main window. Again, if you scroll through the file list, you will see a number of directories listed. The information you want may be contained in one of them. Since you are looking for information about the project, you should begin your search by looking in directories with names appropriate to your search. "Articles" looks like a good directory in which to start because it implies text descriptions. With short FTP titles, finding information is a trial and error process.

Change the working directory to the "Articles" directory. Scroll through the file list and view a few of the files available. With some exploring you will find the information you are looking for in the file "suggest.gut."

Now perhaps you want to keep a copy of this file. Move back to the main Fetch window. To transfer a file to your computer, all you need to do is double-click on the file's name in the file list (or highlight the file name and press the "Get

File . . ." button in the Fetch window). Fetch will present you with a standard save dialogue box so you can select the folder on your computer in which you wish to save the file. At the right-hand side of the main Fetch window you can monitor the rate at which the transfer is progressing. When the transfer is complete, you can continue to explore the directories maintained by this host.

There is something more you should know about file transfer. Different types of files require different types of transfer. In the main Fetch window are three radio buttons labeled "Automatic," "Text," and "Binary." If you know what type of file you are going to transfer, you should select the appropriate button. If you leave the "Automatic" button activated, however, Fetch will guess as to the type of file transfer required. For more information on file types and how they relate to FTP, see the box "File Troubleshooting" later in this chapter.

Congratulations. You have just completed your first file transfer using Fetch. But you are not quite done yet. You still need to close your connection with the FTP host. To do this, simply select the "Close Connection" button in the upper right-hand corner of the main Fetch window.

Fetch is a wonderfully written, well-supported program with extensive built-in help. In order to learn more about Fetch and its many powerful options, be sure to read the "Fetch Help" information available in the menu of the program itself.

A SAMPLE UNIX FTP SESSION

UNIX-based FTP programs like the one in this example are available for use at virtually all Internet sites, regardless of how advanced their services are. While this is much less user friendly than gopher FTP or network applications like Fetch, it is useful for a well-educated Internet user to be familiar with the rough and direct way of using FTP, not only to allow the user to be prepared for unusual situations, but also to give the user a better idea about how FTP works. In this sample session we will again connect with the anonymous FTP host at the University of Iowa at Urbana-Champaign where Project Gutenberg electronic texts are housed. We will obtain an index of those documents.

This example should give you a good feel for some of the basic commands of a UNIX FTP session. An actual FTP session would appear as a continuous dialogue on your computer screen. To simplify this demonstration, however, the FTP session has been divided into small blocks, each following on explanation of a step in the session.

Begin by logging in to your time-sharing account. At the command prompt (usually represented by a $ or a %), type **FTP.** Your local system will run its FTP program.

```
$ ftp
MultiNet ftp user process 3.3(109)
```

Next, type **open,** followed by a space and either the name or the numerical IP address of the remote host to which you wish to connect. It is important to note that most sites will respond to either the name or the numerical address, but occasionally a site will respond only to a numerical address. The address we are going to use in this example is **mrcnext.cso.uiuc.edu,** an anonymous FTP host at the University of Iowa at Urbana-Champaign, where the files of Project Gutenberg are stored. Once you have entered the address, and press <ENTER>, if the remote site is active, you will be connected.

```
ftp>open
To foreign host: mrcnext.cso.uiuc.edu
Connection opened (Assuming 8-bit connections)
<mrcnext.cso.uiuc.edu ftp server (Version wu-2.4(1)
Mon Sep 5 19:43:28 CDT 1994) ready.
```

Now you need to tell the host who you are. Some sites will prompt you for a password and user name when you first log on. Others require you to issue the "user" command to ask for a user name prompt.

```
MRCNEXT.CSO.UIUC.EDU>user
```

When the remote machine asks for your user name, enter **anonymous.** Some hosts limit the number of anonymous FTP users; if the number of connections has already reached the maximum, you will be asked to try again later.

For your password, you are generally asked to enter your e-mail address (**me@where.I.am**). However, some systems may require that you enter **guest** or **new.** Entering your e-mail address is a courtesy for those sites that like to know who is making use of their facility.

```
Foreign username: anonymous
<Guest login ok, send your complete e-mail address as
password.
Password: me@where.I.am
<Mail comments or suggestions to
jgross@mrcnext.cso.uiuc.edu.
```

The remote host will respond with some basic information regarding transfer and connection policies, and in this case the host also explains that the Gutenberg archives (the most popular item at this site) are located in the directory **/pub/etext.**

```
<--> You are user 66 out of 75 allowed in your usage class.
<*** All transfers are logged with your host name and email
address.
<*** If you don't like this policy, disconnect now!
<
<*** The Gutenberg archives are located in    /pub/etext
<*** GNU software is being mirrored in        /pub/gnu
<*** Tons of MACUG stuff is in                /pub/mac
<*** PCSIG stuff is in                        /pub/pcsig
<*** Check out the new LINUX archives in      /pub/linux
<*** New INFO-MAC mirror in                   /pub/info-mac
<*** Cica Windows archive in                  /pub/win3
<
< UIUC Linux users can now do network installations.
  Download the README
< file from /pub/linux/UIUC/netinstall for more information.
<
<Please read the file /README
< it was last modified on Fri Nov 18 12:52:54 1994
  - 54 days ago
<Guest login ok, access restrictions apply.
```

Since you are looking for information about Project Gutenberg, you should use the command **cd /pub/etext.** This will change the remote working directory to the directory that contains the Project Gutenberg files. What should you do if you don't know what directory to go to to find the information you need? Most sites will maintain a README file in the root directory (the directory in which you begin the session). This file contains information about the site and the directories it contains. If README is not helpful or does not exist, then you may need to explore the directories until you find the information you are looking for.

```
MRCNEXT.CSO.UIUC.EDU>cd pub/etext
<CWD command successful.
```

In order to see the contents of this new directory, you should issue the **dir** command. This will return a lengthy listing of all the files and directories accessible through this directory.

```
MRCNEXT.CSO.UIUC.EDU>dir
```

Now you have the opportunity to check for system notices containing special information relevant to this directory. Begin by looking for any README files or Index files. These files are likely to contain messages about the location, size, and purpose of different files within the directory. The first one listed in the example is "0index.gut."

```
<Opening ASCII mode data connection for /bin/ls.
total 137
-rw-r—r— 1 root      wheel    191 Mar 20 1994 .dir3_0.wmd
-rw-r—r— 1 root      wheel    11 Mar 20 1994 .hidden
-rw-r—r— 1 hart      wheel    26517 Jan 11 10:00 0INDEX.GUT
-rw-r—r— 1 hart      wheel    9188 Dec 12 22:39 INDEX100.GUT
-rw-r—r— 1 hart      wheel    7086 Dec 12 22:24 INDEX200.GUT
-rw-r—r— 1 hart      wheel    703 Dec 12 22:26 INDEX400.GUT
-rw-r—r— 1 hart      wheel    9214 Jan 15 1990 LIST.COM
-rw-r—r— 1 hart      wheel    4420 Dec 1 1991 NEWUSER.GUT
drwxr-xr-x 3 hart     wheel    1024 Nov 1 20:31 articles
drwxr-xr-x 2 hart     wheel    1024 Dec 10 1993 etext90
drwxr-xr-x 2 hart     wheel    2048 Dec 10 17:13 etext91
drwxr-xr-x 2 hart     wheel    2048 Dec 30 00:11 etext92
drwxr-xr-x 2 hart     wheel    4096 Dec 16 20:45 etext93
drwxr-xr-t 3 hart     wheel    4096 Dec 12 22:27 etext94
drwxr-xr-x 2 hart     wheel    2048 Jan 9 21:43 etext95
drwxr-xr-x 2 hart     wheel    1024 Aug 4 1993 freenet
drwxr-xr-x 6 hart     wheel    1024 Jan 13 1994 hart
drwxr-xr-x 7 ippe     wheel    1024 Jan 11 11:44 ippe
drwxr-xr-x 2 root     wheel    8192 Mar 1 1994 lost+found
-rw-r—r— 1 hart      wheel    51276 Sep 21 10:07 o640.gif
<Transfer complete.
```

Now you will need to retrieve the file so that you can read it. In order to transfer the file properly, you will need to set the type of file transfer to **ascii.** This tells your local FTP client that you are going to be transferring files that are only text. (For more information on file transfer types, see "File Troubleshooting" later in this chapter.)

```
MRCNEXT.CSO.UIUC.EDU>ascii
Type: Ascii (Non-Print), Structure: File, Mode: Stream
```

You are now ready to transfer the file. Issue the "get" command followed by a space and the name of the file you wish to transfer. Remember that UNIX is case sensitive, so if a file name is capitalized in the directory list, you should capitalize it when you type your request. Therefore, you would type **get 0INDEX.GUT** for this example. The next line is a prompt for the name you wish to save the file under on your local system. After you name the file, the transfer will begin.

```
MRCNEXT.CSO.UIUC.EDU>get 0INDEX.GUT
To local file: 0index.gut
<Opening ASCII mode data connection for 0INDEX.GUT (26517
bytes).
<Transfer complete.
```

Here you may want to exit the FTP program for a moment and use your text editor to view the document you have just retrieved (to exit, issue the "close" and "quit" commands).

```
MRCNEXT.CSO.UIUC.EDU>close
<Goodbye.
ftp>quit
$
```

You will quickly realize that this file is not a lot of help. It contains information but no explanation of what that information is. Perhaps another index would be more helpful. Restart the FTP program and reconnect to **mrcnext.cso.uiuc.edu.** Move to the directory **/pub/etext** and use the "get" command to retrieve the file "INDEX100.GUT." Exit FTP and take a look at this file. It is much more useful. It not only contains an index of some of the files available through Project Gutenberg, but it also contains an explanation of the file "0INDEX.GUT": It is a smaller index, updated daily.

```
MRCNEXT.CSO.UIUC.EDU>get INDEX100.GUT
 To local file: INDEX100.GUT
<Opening ASCII mode data connection for INDEX100.GUT (9188
 bytes).
<Transfer complete.
MRCNEXT.CSO.UIUC.EDU>close
<Goodbye.
ftp>quit
$
```

Once again, connect to **mrcnext.cso.uiuc.edu.** Move into the **/pub/etext** directory and look at the directory list again. Now that you have an idea of the type of resources available through Project Gutenberg, you will probably want some information on how to access those resources. With a little exploration you will find the file suggest.gut located in the directory **/pub/etext/articles.** This file can be retrieved by the same process as the other titles were above. It contains information about downloading the texts created by Project Gutenberg.

```
MRCNEXT.CSO.UIUC.EDU>cd articles
<CWD command successful.
MRCNEXT.CSO.UIUC.EDU>dir
<Opening ASCII mode data connection for /bin/ls.
total 460
-rw-r-r- 1 hart    wheel    14970 Nov 29 1993 0INDEX.GUT
-rw-r-r- 1 hart    wheel    9189 Jan 1 1994 INDEX100.GUT
-rw-r-r- 1 hart    wheel    5821 Sep 4 07:24 INDEX200.GUT
-rw-r-r- 1 hart    wheel    4420 Mar 23 1992 NEWUSER.GUT
-rw-r-r- 1 hart    wheel    1902 Jul 12 1993 SHORT.FAQ
-rw-r-r- 1 hart    wheel    2473 Oct 6 1993 blurb.gut
-rw-r-r- 1 hart    wheel    4006 Jul 6 1993 copyrite.rul
drwxr-xr-x 2 hart wheel    3072 Mar 2 1994 gut-logs
```

```
-rw-r-r- 1 hart     wheel    9287 Jan 18 1994 gut94
-rw-r-r- 1 hart     wheel    8670 Jul 31 16:46 gutjul.94
-rw-r-r- 1 hart     wheel    22423 Nov 2 1993 gutnov.93
-rw-r-r- 1 hart     wheel    16784 Oct 21 1993 gutoct.93
-rw-r-r- 1 hart     wheel    16162 Mar 30 1991 harvard.ota
-rw-r-r- 1 hart     wheel    29405 Mar 30 1991 highways.apl
-rw-r-r- 1 hart     wheel    25891 Aug 9 1992 history.gut
-rw-r-r- 1 hart     wheel    5422 Nov 5 1992 incoming.gut
-rw-r-r- 1 hart     wheel    18383 Feb 21 1994 inerap93.art
-rw-r-r- 1 hart     wheel    4420 Feb 1 1992 new.gut
-rw-r-r- 1 hart     wheel    96506 Mar 17 1992 nren.txt
-rw-r-r- 1 hart     wheel    51276 Sep 21 10:07 o640.gif
-rw-r-r- 1 hart     wheel    41879 Nov 1 19:12 progress
-rw-r-r- 1 incoming incoming 8226 Oct 19 19:11 savenet.994
-rw-r-r- 1 hart     wheel    5036 Apr 11 1994 standard.494
-rw-r-r- 1 hart     wheel    23356 Dec 8 1993 standard.d93
-rw-r-r- 1 hart     wheel    23178 Oct 23 1993 standard.gut
-rw-r-r- 1 hart     wheel    4959 Nov 5 1992 suggest.gut
-rw-r-r- 1 hart     wheel    2351 Jan 17 1994 www.$
<Transfer complete.
MRCNEXT.CSO.UIUC.EDU>get suggest.gut
 To local file: suggest.gut
<Opening ASCII mode data connection for suggest.gut (4959
bytes).
 <Transfer complete.
```

Just a reminder. Whenever you wish to exit the FTP program, you should go through the following steps. Issue the "close" command to tell FTP to close its link to the remote host, and then type **quit** to exit FTP and return to the command prompt.

```
MRCNEXT.CSO.UIUC.EDU>close
<Goodbye.
ftp>quit
$
```

COMMON FTP COMMANDS

For most UNIX, VM, and VMS machines, the command to start the FTP program is **FTP** (or **ftp**). Once you are inside the program, you can get a list of the FTP commands in brief by typing **help** or **?**. Personal computer communication programs, and in particular the graphically-oriented programs used with SLIP or PPP connections, may use a variety of commands to run FTP. Fortunately, these programs usually contain documentation explaining their commands and procedures for their use. The following list of commands should be sufficient for most non-geographically-oriented programs:

`ftp`	Start an FTP session.
`lcd`	Local change of directory (change to the directory you want to save to).
`open (the.ftp.host.name)`	Access the named FTP host (e.g., **mrc-next.cso.uiuc.edu**).
`dir`	Display the contents of a directory (verbose listing).
`ls`	Display the contents of a directory (usually a brief listing).
`cd`	Change directory.
`cd. . .`	Change directory up one level (UNIX hosts).
`cd[-]`	Change directory up one level (VMS hosts).
`ascii`	Prepare FTP for text-only transfer.
`binary or bin`	Prepare FTP for a binary file transfer.
`get (filename)`	Copy a file from an FTP host to your home system.
`get (filename) -`	If you place a space and a hyphen after the filename, and then press <ENTER>, the remote system may display the text file. Refer to your local on-line manual ("man FTP") pages for more information.
`get (filename) "!more"`	Send the file to the "more" command (a common text reader on most time-sharing systems). This will allow you to read the file, pressing a key to move from page to page. Refer your local "man ftp" and "man more" pages for information about this command.
`user`	On some FTP clients, you may need to issue the "user" command if you are not automatically asked for a user name at the beginning of the FTP session.
`close`	Close connection to the remote host without quitting FTP.
`quit or bye`	Quit ftp.

FILE TROUBLESHOOTING

You will find when using FTP that occasionally there are files that seem unusual in format. The file may not appear when you try to view it, or you may not be able to view it at all. If it is a piece of software that you have downloaded, it may not run. Before you write the problem off as an error during transfer or a corrupted file, there are a few things that you may want to think about:

Transfer Type: Ascii or Binary?

When using FTP, you have to set the transfer type to either ascii or binary. You do this by giving the command **ascii** or **binary.** So what are they? ASCII is a text-only format. Many files that need to be transferred in this mode will have filenames ending in **.txt** or **.wpd.** However, any file that you expect to contain just text (an electronic journal, an RFC sheet, a FAQ list, etc.) should be transferred via the ASCII format.

Binary files are nontext files (such as software, graphics, digitized sounds, compressed files, and archive files) which have been stored in binary code to allow them to be transmitted over the Internet. Whenever you transfer a file of this type, you should set the transfer type to **binary.** If you transfer it via ASCII, the file will be corrupted and not be usable.

Archived File Groups

When several files belong together, like chapters in a document or like software and its documentation, often they will be bundled together in one file called an archive. The archived file is given one name, which makes it easy to FTP. After you have transferred the files, you must remove them from the archive before you can use them (see the following explanation of compressed files). Many archived files have an extension such as **.tar** at the end of the filename, which allows you to recognize them.

Compressed Files

Many files stored at FTP sites are compressed. Compressed files are files that have been run through a special translation program that makes them take up less storage space. File compression also allows files to be transferred around the Internet much faster. There are a variety of programs available to uncompress compressed files. Unfortunately, there are many different types of file compression, so it may be difficult to determine what program to use to uncompress a file that you have transferred. Compressed files can be identified by the extension on the end of their filename, for example, **.Z, .zip,** or **.arj.**

For more information on using these programs, contact your system administrator and also read any local help file or on-line manual pages pertaining to these subjects. Many FTP sites also explain file decoding in one of the README files in their archives.

So, before you delete a document or piece of software that does not seem to work properly, try some of these options and see whether or not you can correct the problem.

HOW DO YOU FIND FTP SITES?

FTP may be the easiest method for retrieving information on the Internet *if you know where a file is located*. So how do you know?

1. You can read about files in books or articles about the Internet.
2. You can explore FTP sites that seem likely with hopes of stumbling across the information you need.
3. Or you can use Archie, the key word search tool for FTP which is discussed just after the following list of FTP sites.

INTERESTING FTP SITES

To use the following addresses, access your FTP client and type the address. For example, from a UNIX FTP client, you would need to type FTP before each of the addresses; if you browse around in these sites, you will find other helpful information.

Apple Support Information
ftp.apple.com

Books
Project Gutenberg*
mrcnext.cso.uiuc.edu (/pub/etext)

Dante Project
ftp.dartmouth.edu

U.S. federal government information.
ftp.spies.com
Historical and current documents and other information.

Internet Hunt
ftp.cic.net (/pub/internet-hunt)
A monthly scavenger hunt for facts and trivia on and about the Net.

Internet Book Information Center
sunsite.unc.edu (/pub/docs)

Library Catalogs and Databases
ftp.unt.edu (/libraries/libraries.txt)
Instructions on how to access computerized library systems of many universities around the world.

Macintosh Software and Archive
ftp.utexas.edu (/pub/mac)

Privacy and Anonymity Issues
rtfm.mit.edu (/pub/usenet/news.answers/
net-privacy)

*At press time the address was changed to **uiarchive.cso.uiuc.edu** (/pub/etext).

Software (many computer types)
ftp.cdrom.com

Social Sciences
coombs.anu.edu.au

Travel
ftp.cc.umanitoba.ca (/rec-travel)
Travelogues, guides, FAQs.

ARCHIE

Archie is a program that functions as a catalog and index of FTP archives. The Archie program, using a master list, periodically searches all known FTP sites on the Internet and stores the filenames in a central database which is available for you to search. All you need to do is contact one of the Archie servers and ask it whether your information is available and, if so, where you should go to find it. When you contact Archie, you ask it to look in its files for a particular "string of characters"; it will search its database and return a list of all files that contain that string and also the address of the computer(s) to contact and the directories containing the files.

How do you find this wonderful resource? You can access and use Archie in several ways. You may find an Archie client on your university's system, or, if your university doesn't have one, you can Telnet to an Archie server for your search. Or you can use an Archie client at one of the gopher FTP sites mentioned earlier in this chapter.

Telnetting to Archie

To access Archie by Telnet, choose an Archie server from the list at the end of the chapter and, at your system's command prompt, type:

```
telnet archie.internic.net (or other Archie server)
```

When prompted to do so, log in as "archie" and press <ENTER>. You are now connected to the Archie server.

There are three types of Archie searches. Ninety-nine percent of them are name searches. In this type of search you enter the name of the file or program that you are looking for and Archie will tell you where it can be found.

Some FTP sites maintain a file description database; since many filenames do not accurately reflect the contents of the file, you can use Archie to search these databases for descriptions of files. Only a small fraction of FTP sites maintain this type of database, and so this type of search is not frequently used.

Finally, Archie offers a site search feature, which allows you to get information about specific hosts monitored by Archie. In this way you can search for hosts on the basis of part of an Internet address. For example, you could search for hosts in a particular country if you knew the extension of the address used by sites in that country.

Archie Name Search Commands

When you telnet to an Archie server to do a name search, the first command you should enter is **show search.** You will then be told which type of name search the Archie server is set up to perform. There are four types of name search. To change the search type, you issue the command **set search** followed by the name of the search type you wish to perform.

set search exact	This is a case-sensitive string search. It will look for exactly what you input and nothing else.
set search subcase	This is a case-sensitive substring search. If you were to search for the name "wire," for example, the search would return items such as **wired** and **little.wire** but would not return **Big.Wire** or **Wired.**
set search sub	This is the most common search type because it is the broadest. It is a case-insensitive substring search. If you were to search for the name "wire," for example, the search would return items such as **Big.Wire, Wire, wired,** and **little.wire.**
set search regex	This search is done just like the UNIX command **regex.** It is a sophisticated search method that involves wildcards and other tricks. For more information about regex searches, check your local on-line manual pages or consult your help desk.

Help is never more than a few keystrokes away. When you are connected to an Archie server via Telnet, you can always type **help** for more information on something you are confused about.

You are finally ready to enter the search term. The command you use is **prog,** though newer Archie servers may also accept the command **find.** This command should be followed by the name of the item you wish to search for. For example, if you want to find the word "mechanical" and want the broadest search possible, you begin by telneting to an Archie server and making sure that it was set for a **sub** search; if it were not, you would issue the command **set search sub.** Next you type **prog mechanical.** The Archie server would begin its search, and in a few moments it would present you with a list of all of the locations where it had found the word "mechanical" in a filename.

ARCHIE SITES

The following is a list of addresses for initiating Archie searches. You can tel-net to any of these sites to begin your Archie search.

archie.ac.il	archie.nz
archie.ans.net	archie.rutgers.edu
archie.au	archie.switch.ch
archie.doc.ic.ac.uk	archie.unipi.it
archie.funet.fi	archie.univie.ac.at
archie.luth.se	archie.unl.edu
archie.ncu.edu.tw	archie.wide.ad.jp

ASSIGNMENTS

1. FTP to Project Gutenberg and obtain a current index of documents.
2. Explore the list of popular FTP sites via gopher that appears on the University of Illinois at Urbana-Champaign gopher, **gopher.uiuc.edu.** Write a memo describing the contents of the gophers you can access through that option.
3. By consulting various Internet directories at the reference desk of your university library, construct an annotated list of FTP sites that are relevant to your major. With each FTP site include a brief description of the documents available.

QUESTIONS TO ASK

1. How do you access an FTP client on your university's system? (This will vary according to the kind of system your university has and any shell programs run by the system.)
2. What are some of the other basic commands that are used to run FTP at your site? For example, do you type **FTP (site name)** at the command prompt? Or do you type **FTP** <ENTER>, and then **open (site name)?**
3. Are you actually able to view documents via FTP, or must you download them first? If it is possible to view them, what are the commands required?
4. How do you download files via FTP? How do you transfer them to your hard disk (or floppy disk) if a transfer is necessary?
5. Does your university have an Archie client? If so, how do you access it?

T E N

TELNET

WHAT IS TELNET?

Telnet is an Internet protocol which makes it possible for you to log on to a remote computer and manipulate it as if you were physically present. Why is this important? It gives you real-time access to libraries, databases, and other types of information servers throughout the world. Some Telnet sites can be reached via gopher, appearing on major gopher site menus, while some can be reached only by telnetting directly.

The two most common uses of Telnet are guest Telnet and full privilege Telnet. Full privilege Telnet allows you to log in to a computer on which you have a regular account, a user name, and a password. For example, let's say John has two e-mail accounts, one on a machine named Musica and the other on a machine named Octavia. If he is logged in on Musica and wants to see if he has any new mail on Octavia, he would Telnet to Octavia, put in his user name and password, and look for new mail just as if he had been logged on to Octavia.

Guest Telnet allows you to log in to a computer through a special guest account from which you can use predefined services on the remote machine, such as browsing a library catalog or searching a database. Guest Telnet is available to anyone.

HOW DO YOU USE TELNET?

First you need to access Telnet software. As with gopher and other protocols, how you do this depends on the type of connection and computer you are using. In many cases you simply type at the command line or prompt, **telnet** followed by the host name of the computer you wish to contact. With a UNIX system you may need to type **telnet** <ENTER>, then **open (host name).** If you have point-and-click access to Internet protocols, you may need only to "double-click" on the Telnet screen icon. As was described in Chapter 2 and elsewhere, point-and-click access is likely available if you have a SLIP or PPP connection or if you are using Windows or a Macintosh in a university computer lab.

The Telnet address is nothing more than the host name of the machine you wish to contact. If you remember the discussion of e-mail addresses in Chapter 3, you will recall that a host name consists of wordlike letters separated by periods. For example, the Telnet address for the Federal Information Exchange Inc. (FEDIX) is **fedix.fie.com.** Occasionally the host name is followed by a port number (usually a two-digit number), such as **liberty.uc.wlu.edu 70,** the host name and port for the gopher host at Washington and Lee University. A port number may be necessary because of the multi-user nature of time-sharing computers: Some parts of the computer can be accessed only through certain gateways, or ports. All Telnet addresses, like other Internet addresses, have numeric equivalents. If you have both a host name address and a numeric address, you can use either (if you find the host name address doesn't work, try the numeric if you have it).

After you connect, the remote computer will ask you for a login and password. This information is usually listed along with the host name of the site (such as in one of the on-line lists of Telnet resources or in published Internet books). Some sites provide this information before the login prompt as a courtesy.

Once you are connected, the remote computer will give you some information which may include an escape character, or combination of keystrokes to use when you want to exit the remote site. At this point the remote machine may also inform you of use policies, special commands, or time limits for your session. This information is important, so read it carefully.

The remote site may ask you to set the type of terminal emulation, although many sites will set this for you. Because there are several types of terminals available on the market, and the way they display information may vary, the remote computer is simply asking in what shape and size to send information and what types of responses to expect. The most common type of terminal is the VT100, so you might try that unless instructed otherwise by your instructor or systems operator (you'll know if you have the wrong terminal emulation because either the remote computer will not accept the connection or the text will be received in an unreadable form).

Note: If the remote site is using an IBM mainframe computer, you may need to use a similar program called TN3270 instead of Telnet. TN3270 works essentially like Telnet. To initiate it, with many systems, you simply type **TN3270** instead of **telnet,** followed by the site address.

Telnet is the one protocol that has no standard set of commands. All commands beyond logging in to the remote machine are determined by the administrators of the remote machine. Commands for downloading, saving, and processing information will vary from site to site. Some sites have extensive on-line help and documentation to guide you through their resources, while others may be more difficult to use.

SAMPLE TELNET SESSION

Carl UnCover, a database which indexes thousands of academic journals, is a menu item on many university gophers, but it can also be accessed directly via Telnet. Type the following at your system command prompt:

```
telnet database.carl.org
```

Press <ENTER>, and you will receive this screen, which welcomes you to CARL and asks for your terminal type:

```
Welcome to the CARL system
Please identify your terminal. Choices are:
1. ADM (all)
2. APPLE, IBM
3. TANDEM
4. TELE-914
5. VT100
6. WYSE 50
7. ZENTEC
8. HARDCOPY
9. IBM 316x

Use HARDCOPY if your terminal type isn't listed.

SELECT LINE #
```

Despite what CARL tells you, unless you have been instructed otherwise by your instructor or system professional, try VT100 (the most common type) by selecting option 5. This is the next screen:

```
        WELCOME TO THE CARL CORPORATION NETWORK AND UNCOVER
CARL Corporation is proud to present our Shopping List of Data-
bases. Many of the databases included require a password and a
licensing fee. If you have already paid your license and have a
password  to  a  database,  please  enter  your  password  when
prompted. There are a number of library catalogs and free data-
bases available, please feel free to look around. Please contact
CARL Corporation at database@carl.org or 303/758-3030 for more
information on licensing.

1.    UnCover
      (Article Access and Delivery)
2.    Information Access Company Databases
      (including Business Index, Magazine Index and others)
3.    Grolier's Academic American Encyclopedia
4.    Facts on File
5.    H.W. Wilson Databases (including Library Literature)
6.    UMI Databases (including ABI/Inform)
7.    Other information and Article Databases
      (including Journal Graphics, Choice and others)
8.    CARL Systems Library Catalogs

You may enter //EXIT at any time to leave this system.
Enter the NUMBER of your choice, and press the <RETURN> key>>
```

As you can see, CARL offers a variety of databases, some free and some requiring a fee. You want option 1, UnCover, so type that at the prompt. Next CARL tells you that you can enter a password and receive a discounted rate on article delivery. This means that you can order articles directly from CARL for a fee, and they will be faxed to you. You are not required to do this to use CARL. Press <ENTER> and the next screen will give you directions about types of searches.

```
                         Welcome to
                          UnCover

              The Article Access and Delivery Solution

UnCover contains records describing journals and their contents. Over
4000 current citations are added daily. UnCover offers you the opportu-
nity to order fax copies of articles from this database.
```

```
To use UnCover, enter:     W for WORD or TOPIC search
                           N for AUTHOR search
                           B for BROWSE by journal title
For information, type      ? to learn about UnCover
                           ?C to learn about UnCover Complete
                           ?R to learn about UnCover Reveal ALERT service
                           QS to learn about searching short-cuts
To leave UnCover, type     S to STOP or SWITCH to another database
Type the letter (s) of the UnCover service you want and press <RETURN>
                           SELECTED DATABASE: UnCover
```

Select **w** for a word search and receive an explanation that word searches can mean words from titles, summaries or abstracts, table of contents, names of people. This is a little different from the way searches are organized in traditional library catalogs.

You will be searching for articles about "telnet," so type that word at the prompt. The following screen lists the number of "hits" for the search.

```
1 TELNET
      9 ITEMS
2 TELNETTING
      1 ITEM
ALL ITEMS HAVE BEEN DISPLAYED.
ENTER <LINE NUMBER(S)> TO DELETE TERM(S)--(separate numbers with commas)
<Q>UIT for NEW SEARCH.
```

CARL found nine items on Telnet and one on Telnetting. As directed, enter line number 1 to list the articles. CARL gives you enough information that you can order articles through interlibrary loan, if you so choose. Sometimes CARL also gives a brief article abstract.

The information that you can obtain from CARL can be extremely helpful for a term paper or other research project because it indexes so many academic and professional journals. In addition to searching for subject, you can request the table of contents for a specific journal issue, which is helpful if you want to learn what are current topics in a particular field.

```
┌─────────────────────────────────────────────────────────────────────┐
│                                                                       │
│                    TYPICAL TELNET COMMANDS                            │
│                                                                       │
│     Ctrl+]        Escape character.                                   │
│     Close         Ends Telnet session, terminating connection to      │
│                   remote computer.                                    │
│     Open          When at the Telnet prompt, "open" followed by a     │
│                   site address will initiate a Telnet session.        │
│     Quit          Terminates connection to remote site and ends       │
│                   Telnet session.                                     │
│     set echo      Use if you cannot see what you are typing or if     │
│                   your typing appears double. A toggle switch.        │
│     display       Shows current parameters or settings.               │
│     set ?         See list of operating parameters or settings you    │
│                   can control with a set command. Check this if you   │
│                   are having problems manipulating the remote         │
│                   computer.                                           │
│                                                                       │
└─────────────────────────────────────────────────────────────────────┘
```

FINDING TELNET SITES

Information about Telnet sites, like that for other types of Internet sites, can be found in reference books about the Internet or in lists on the Internet itself (see the Appendix for a list of on-line resources). Information about Telnet sites, however, is perhaps a little harder to find than that for some other protocols because the access interface for a number of sites has moved to gopher or the WWW. For example, if you want to browse libraries in California, the easiest way is to use gopher or the WWW to access the Telnet links to the libraries. In other words, many users probably aren't going to set out to find new Telnet sites; rather, when they are looking for a resource about a certain topic, they may find that the link to the resource is via Telnet. Thus, you need to have a basic knowledge of Telnet to maximize your ability to use the Internet as a research resource.

Browser

Hytelnet (or hypertext browser for Telnet-accessible sites on the Internet) is an Internet program which is useful for finding addresses and log-in procedures for Telnet sites. It is available at several gopher sites including **liberty.uc.wlu.edu** (/Explore Internet Resources/Telnet Login to Sites Hytelnet). On the WWW, Hytelnet can be found at **http://www.usask.ca/cgi-bin/hytelnet.**

Library Catalogs

More and more major libraries are making their catalogs available on-line, allowing you to search their holdings, though usually not actual books, periodicals, or other materials. Several gophers offer menu access to Telnet connections for libraries around the world. Try gopher **libgopher.yale.edu,** gopher **liberty.uc.wlu.edu** (/Libraries and Information Access/Library Catalogs—Major Research Institutions), and gopher **yaleinfo.yale.edu** (/Browse Yaleinfo/Library Catalogs World-wide).

Also, lists of library Telnet addresses and passwords can be downloaded from FTP sites. Try ftp **ftp.unt.edu** (/library) or ftp **dla.ucop.edu** (/pub/internet/libcat-guide).

INTERESTING TELNET SITES

The following large data bases and libraries can be accessed via Telnet. For many systems, type **telnet (sitename).**

Federal Information Exchange Inc. (FEDIX)
   fedix.fie.com

Food and Drug Administration
   fdabbs.fda.gov (log-in **bbs**)
   News releases, drug and device product approvals list, text of testimony at FDA Congressional hearings, etc.

Free-Nets
   Telnet access through Hytelnet via
    http;//www.usask.ca/cgi-bin/hytelnet
   (/Other Telnet accessible services)

Geography
   martini.eecs.umich.edu 3000
   Population, latitude and longitude, elevation, annual rainfall, time zone, and other information on cities and regions of the United States.

History
   ukanaix.cc.ukans.edu (log-in **history**)
   Hypertext history database.

Internet Resources
   NICOL (Network Information Center On-Line)
   nicol.jvnc.net (log-in **nicol**)
   Information about Internet library resources, Internet Society, and Internet pro-

tocols, as well as databases for medical resources, publishers on-line, and educational services. (Also on gopher at **nicol.jvnc.net.**)

Library Catalogs (through gopher)
> gopher **libgopher.yale.edu**
> gopher **liberty.uc.wlu.edu** (/Libraries and Information Access/Library Catalogs—Major Research Institutions)
> gopher **yaleinfo.yale.edu** (/Browse Yaleinfo/Library Catalogs World-wide).

Library Catalogs (through Hytelnet)
> gopher **liberty.uc.wlu.edu** (/Explore Internet Resources >Hytelnet) *or* **http://www.usask.ca/cgi-bin/hytelnet**

Library of Congress
> **locis.loc.gov**
> Library of Congress catalog, federal legislation, copyright information, and foreign law.

NASA Spacelink
> **spacelink.msfc.nasa.gov** (log-in **guest**)
> Lesson plans for math, science, engineering, and technology; current status reports on NASA projects, NASA educational publications, and other educational materials related to the space program.

Stock Market
> **a2i.rahul.net** (log-in **guest**)
> Daily stock market report (/current system information/market report).

ASSIGNMENTS

1. Do a sample subject search in CARL on a topic of your choice. Compile a bibliography of ten articles on that subject.
2. Consulting other Internet resource books or on-line guides, compile a list of Telnet sites related to your major or other interest. Explore several sites and report your results to the class in an oral report.

QUESTIONS TO ASK

1. How do you access Telnet from your university system? Is there more than one way?
2. What type of terminal emulation is recommended?

ELEVEN

WAIS

WHAT IS WAIS?

WAIS stands for Wide Area Information Server. It is a little like Archie and gopher rolled into one. WAIS gives you the ability to perform keyword searches, or searches for specific words, of documents all over the Internet in different type sites. If a search proves fruitful, WAIS creates a menu out of the responses and ranks each response according to how closely it matches your keywords. You can use this menu either to retrieve documents that look interesting or to provide a base for a new search. The information available through WAIS is not as extensive as that obtainable through FTP, gopher, and, more recently, World Wide Web. Yet the number of WAIS–accessible databases is increasing, and WAIS should take its place as one of the valuable tools for navigating the Internet.

WAIS uses the client/server model, which means that you use a WAIS client program to access WAIS servers around the world. There are a number of WAIS client prgrams for computers connected via a network, SLIP, or PPP connection. ElNet winWAIS for Windows, and WAIStation for the Macintosh are both good clients for that type of connection. Users connected directly to a university's time-sharing system that supports WAIS can access it by issuing a **waissearch** command at the command prompt. Many gopher menus and World Wide Web pages link to WAIS clients, and WAIS clients are accessible via Telnet.

WHAT CAN YOU FIND WITH WAIS?

WAIS is particularly adapted to searching complex textual databases. It provides access to on-line books, bibliographies, software catalogs, library catalogs, Internet information, USENET and LISTSERV archives, and various specialized indexes and databases. For the most part, WAIS databases are science and technology oriented, but new servers are added all the time, broadening the number of topics from which WAIS can draw.

HOW DO YOU ACCESS WAIS?

An easy way to begin using WAIS is to access a World Wide Web browser such as Netscape and enter the address for WAIS Inc., which is **http://www.wais.com/newhomepages/surf.html.** From there follow the directions which allow you to conduct a search. See the sample search in the next section.

You can also Telnet to a host that carries a publicly available WAIS client. Telnet to **quake.think.com** and log-in as **wais.** You will be asked to type in a user identifier; use your e-mail address. Once you have done this, the SWAIS (Screen WAIS) client will load. After a few moments it will call up a screen listing a number of WAIS servers. You will need to select one or more servers to be searched. Select those servers that best apply to the subject of your search. To move through the list, you can use the down arrow or **ctrl d.** Use the spacebar to select databases. For more information on a particular database, move to its listing and type **v.** For a more comprehensive list of commands, type **h** or **?.** Once you have picked the servers you want to search, typing **w** will allow you to begin entering keywords.

With WAIS searches, whether through the World Wide Web or Telnet, it is a good idea to start with something broad. If you limit your search, you may unintentionally exclude resources you would find most useful. WAIS ignores a group of words called stop words; these words (such as "a," "the," "etc.") appear so frequently that they are not useful in a search. WAIS also ignores certain buzz words. These words, which vary according to the database, are words that occur so frequently within a particular database that they are not good keywords for a search. You can enter search terms in natural language, and WAIS will search for those words in its databases. If you want to search for a particular phrase such as "free trade agreement," put double quotes around those words, and the query will find only documents with those words in that order.

Once you specify a keyword or words and press <ENTER>, the WAIS client will link to each of the databases you selected and evaluate all of the documents within them, looking for the keywords you specified. WAIS databases all conform to the same conventions for storing data, so it is possible for a WAIS search to evaluate complete documents, unlike other search utilities, which evaluate only titles. Each time a keyword is located, the WAIS client records a hit. When the search is complete, the client will create a menu based on all the hits, including a column of scores, which ranks the items by the frequency that the keywords appear in each document. The highest ranking item is always given a score of 1000, and the other items' scores are based on a percentage of the number of hits in that first item. For example, if you search a database of veterinary journals for the word "catnip," the search might return the names of several articles. The WAIS client would then create a menu listing the articles sorted by the number of hits in each article. The article that uses the word "catnip" the most times would be the first item in the menu and would get a score of 1000. The next article might contain the word only half as many times as the first one and thus would receive a score of 500. Another article farther down the list might contain the word only 10 percent as often as the first and so would receive a score of 100. This scoring system allows you to see quickly which articles have a greater chance of containing the information you need.

SAMPLE WAIS SEARCH

Let's say you would like to find the text to Shakespeare's first sonnet. One method you could try would be to search for Shakespeare's sonnets through a WAIS World Wide Web server and then look for that specific sonnet. Begin by accessing a Web browser such as Netscape. Then type the address for WAIS Inc., which is **http://www.wais.com/newhomepages/surf.html.** You will see a page that tells you a little more about WAIS. Click on the highlighted word "search," and you will see a screen that allows you to enter your keywords. Enter **Shakespeare's sonnets,** and the screen will look like this:

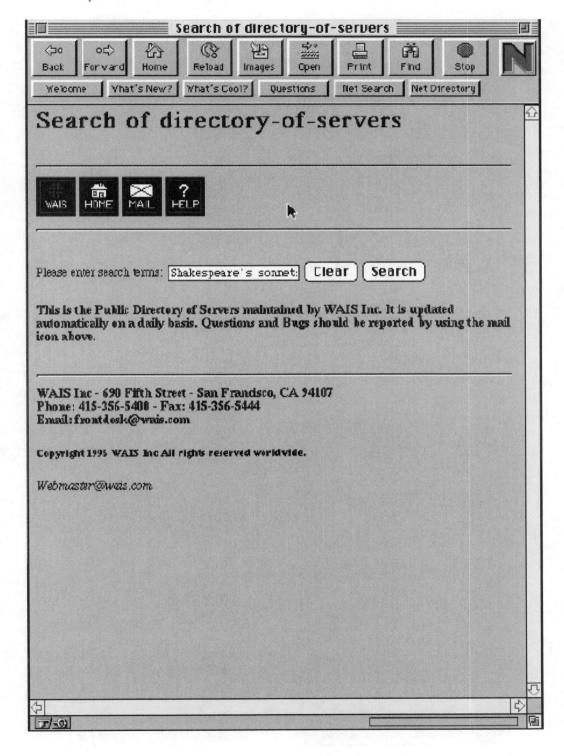

Search of directory-of-servers

Please enter search terms: Shakespeare's sonnet: [**Clear**] [**Search**]

This is the Public Directory of Servers maintained by WAIS Inc. It is updated automatically on a daily basis. Questions and Bugs should be reported by using the mail icon above.

WAIS Inc - 690 Fifth Street - San Francisco, CA 94107
Phone: 415-356-5400 - Fax: 415-356-5444
Email: frontdesk@wais.com

Copyright 1995 WAIS Inc All rights reserved worldwide.

Webmaster@wais.com

Click on "search" and WAIS will search through its databases for those words. After a moment or two you will receive this screen which details the results of the search:

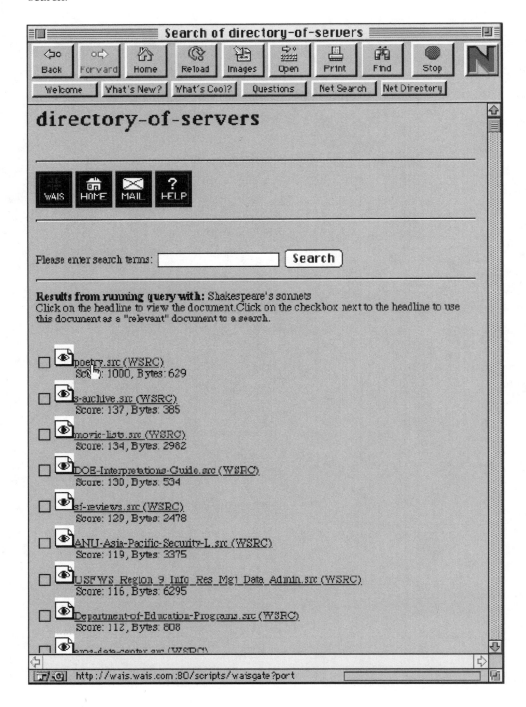

You can now select any of these databases to search further. Click on the high-lighted title of the first database, "poetry.src (WSRC)," for example, since it is the best hit. You will see this screen:

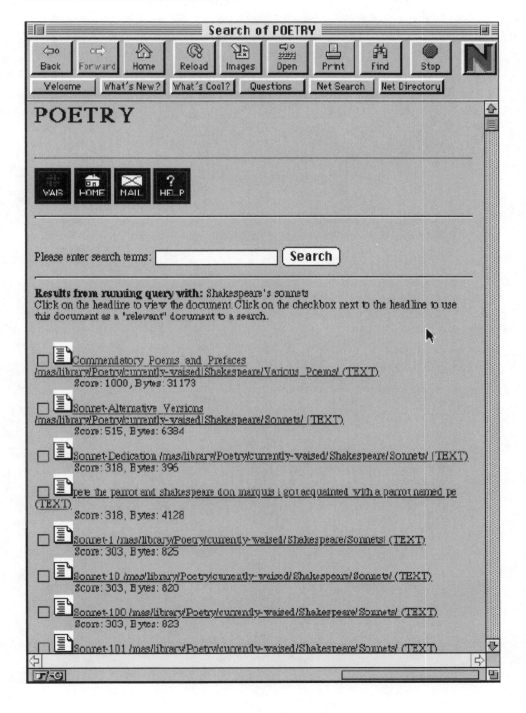

Looking through the list, you see "Sonnet-1." Click on the highlighted title and you will see the following full text of the sonnet:

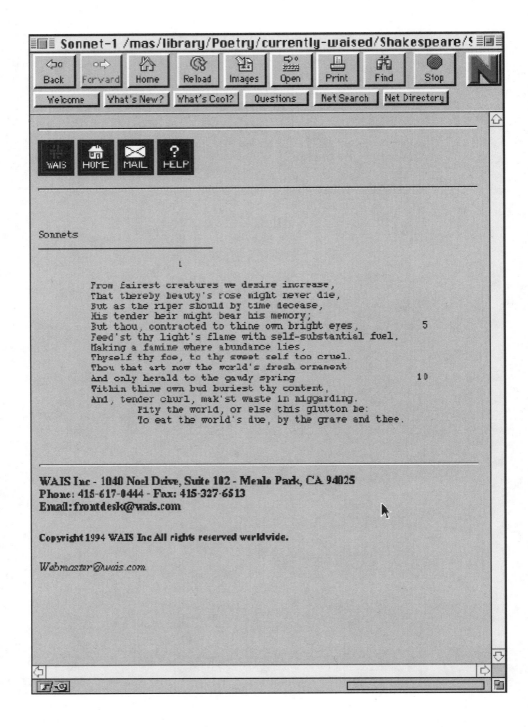

As WAIS searches go, this was a relatively simple one. WAIS requires some trial and error, but it can yield valuable information if you spend a little time learning to work with this powerful tool.

ASSIGNMENTS

1. Determine if your university network offers a WAIS client. If so, use it to do a sample search of a topic suggested by your instructor or one related to your major.
2. Contact the WAIS client at **quake.think.com** or **http://www.wais.com/newhomepages/surf.html** and conduct a sample WAIS search on a topic related to your major or any topic of interest.
3. Explore the FTP site at **quake.think.com** or the Web pages at **http://www.wais.com/newhomepages/surf.html** for information about WAIS. Write a memo about what you learned.

QUESTIONS TO ASK

1. Does your university computer network have a WAIS client installed on it? If so, how do you access it? What are the basic commands?
2. Does your university have a Web page with a WAIS link?
3. Does your university recommend a particular WAIS client program for use with SLIP, PPP, and network connections?
4. Does your university support one of the many WAIS server databases? If so, what kind of information does the local database carry?

T W E L V E

Hints for Searching the Internet

The Internet presents a vast number of widely distributed resources covering thousands of topics and providing many options for research in many different fields. Often there is so much information that you may not know where to begin. Or perhaps you have tried searching for information on a particular topic but simply have not been able to locate what you are looking for. If these problems seem to plague you, this chapter may point you in the right direction.

The Internet is primarily a communication tool. While the type of communications possible is very broad, it all comes down to being able to communicate ideas between people. When searching for information on a particular topic, many people let their past research experiences take over. Traditional methods come to mind, even such methods via a computer. Many people automatically begin with library catalogs or reference materials. These are both good approaches but may not be the best way on the Internet because the Internet is not just static resources but rather is alive with people—real people from all different walks of life and with all kinds of interests and expertise.

One of the best strategies to begin researching a subject via the Internet is to gather advice on where to find information and what information may be useful to you. You can begin by joining one of the over 8,000 USENET newsgroups or one of over 5,000 LISTSERV discussion groups or Internet mailing lists. These give you a chance to put your questions to others who are interested in the same topic, and to give experts a chance to comment on your search and provide answers to many of your questions. These resources will allow you to keep up with the most recent developments in your area of research and may also point you to useful information resources that could have taken a long time to find on your own.

Another good idea is to use the various search engines on the Internet, including the WWW search tools, Veronica, Archie, and WAIS. Through keyword searches, these can help you locate on the Internet data collections that relate to your topic. Or you can search some of the many on-line information guides, some of which are mentioned in the Appendix. An on-line guide is more likely to be up-to-date than its print counterparts, and, because it can be searched quickly by keyword, it reduces the time needed to find what you are looking for. You can also refer to some of the index-type books about the Internet which list resources by topic.

Once you have made some connections and have a good idea of the type and variety of materials available to you, you should start searching for more specific information. Just as with traditional resources, you need to know two things to continue your search: where to find what you are looking for and how to access it. For example, a traditional approach might have started at the card catalog of the university library. After a couple of hours of searching, you might find a few listings that look promising. From the call number of the book, you know where to go to find it. And access is easy: Just read it. But what if it turns out to be stored on microfilm or in a special collection? You need to find out how to access it.

Internet resources are generally accessed with the tools described in this book. Once you have determined where a resource is stored and how to access it, all you have to do is go get it, using the tool that is appropriate to the job. Whether you need to use Telnet, e-mail, FTP, World Wide Web, gopher, WAIS, or some other tool depends on the ways the resource can be accessed; and if it can be accessed several ways, access depends on your personal preference.

Once you have located information, you may want to look around in the same location for more. Information on the Internet is organized, although the location of each subject may seem a bit random (for example, ads for used farm equipment may be available from the same site as are images of surrealistic art). Using broad-based information tools such as gopher and the World Wide Web may help to put the eclectic twistings and turnings of the Net in slightly more apparent order. Nevertheless, you should always spend a moment looking around a site, no matter what tool you used to arrive there. The little clue that brought you to the site may turn out to be the small, exposed end of a gold mine.

Finally, here are a few Internet tips to remember:

1. The Internet is not like a library where information has been categorized and organized with the use of a widely accepted set of rules. It is more like a rummage sale, where items of a similar nature usually get grouped together. In some cases, rather than putting costume jewelry with costume jewelry and old magazines with old magazines, someone will put all of the pink items in one pile and all of the green items in another. While it is organized, the method of organization may not be useful to you.

2. Everything on the Internet has a tendency to be updated, improved, uprooted, relocated, shuffled, cut, and redealt, and otherwise be taken from where it was and replaced or moved to somewhere else. And this happens with some frequency. If you find something that is important to your re-

search, do not expect it to be in the same place tomorrow—or even an hour later. If you find it and need it, keep a copy of it.

3. The Internet is vast. It is made up of hundreds of types of computers, utilizing all kinds of operating systems and connection options. It contains daily contributions from millions of people around the world, all with their own ideas and intellectual and cultural views. No one is an expert on all of the facets of the Internet. While many people are very skilled with the tools and have a good idea where to look for information on many topics, no one can keep up. The Net simply grows and changes too quickly. Fortunately, it is not necessary to understand everything about the Internet to make use of its resources. Perhaps the essential quality needed to navigate the Internet is the willingness to try new avenues of exploration.

APPENDIX

CITING INTERNET SOURCES

The citing of electronic texts from the Internet is such a new concept that formats are still developing, though the most recent *MLA Handbook for Writers of Research Papers, Publication Manual of the American Psychological Association,* and *Chicago Manual of Style* do include brief sections on citing electronic sources. The following sections suggest formats for citing Internet texts which are appropriate for student papers and consistent with the developing MLA (Modern Language Association) and APA (American Psychological Association) style of electronic citations.

MLA Style Format (Modern Language Association)

1. In-text citations

   Citations in the text should refer to a source in the list of works cited. With traditional sources the author's name and the page number are given. However, since electronic documents often do not have authors and since page numbers are generally not consistent, doing this presents a problem. Use the author's name and the page number if they are available. If the list of works cited has more than one work by an author, add the title of the work (or a shortened version if the title is long). If there is no author's name, use the title (or part of it if it is long). If there is no page numbering, use a section number if available.

Examples:

   Jennifer Smith, in her FAQ about MUDS, recommends that participants not use the same password for a character on a MUD as the password on their home system accounts because hackers have been known to gain access to MUD files where passwords are maintained (1.9).

Or:

A FAQ about MUDS recommends that participants not use the same password for a character on a MUD as the password on their home system accounts because hackers have been known to gain access to MUD files where passwords are maintained (Smith 1.9).

2. List of Works Cited

Your primary concern with electronic sources, as with all source materials, should be to give sufficient information that a reader who wishes to do so could retrieve your sources. The problem is that materials on-line are frequently updated, changed, or deleted without notice. When citing an on-line source, you cannot know whether that information will still be in the same form at the same database when a reader might want to refer to it. For this reason, MLA guidelines suggest including the date of access. The following examples list publication date, when available, and access date otherwise.

MLA distinguishes between materials that are on-line versions of printed texts and materials that have no print equivalent. If there is a print version, give that information first in standard MLA format, then give the on-line location where you retrieved the information. If the information is from an on-line database or archive, give the name of the database or archive, if it is available. If the source is an on-line publication, give the title (in italics) after the name of the article in quotes. After the citation, you may give an address and path for the source, preceded by the word "Available."

Electronic mail, according to MLA, should be cited in a manner similar to letters mailed in a conventional manner. If the material cited is from a public on-line posting retrieved by e-mail, include "On-line posting" after the author's name and title of the document.

Examples:

"About Gopher Jewels." 1994. On-line. Internet. 20 March 1995. Available gopher: cwis.usc.edu (/Other Gophers and Information Resources/Gopher-Jewels/Gopher Jewels Information and Help File: About Gopher Jewels. txt).

Fanderclai, Tari Lin. "MUDs in Education: New Environments, New Pedagogies." *Computer–Mediated Communication Magazine* 2.1 (1 Jan. 1995). On-line. Internet. Available World Wide Web: http://sunsite.unc.edu/cmc/mag/ 1995/.

Smith, Jennifer. "Frequently Asked Questions: Basic Information About Muds and Mudding #1." 1994. On-line. Internet. Available FTP: ftp.univie.ac.at (/archive/faq/games/mud-faq/part 1).

Smith, Margaret. E-mail to Ann Jones. 20 March 1995.

Wozniak, Adam Peter. "Doran's Mudlist." On-line posting. Internet. Accessed 14 March 1995. Available E-mail: mudlist@lore.calpoly.edu Message: Mail (in subject line).

APA Style Format (American Psychological Association)

1. In-Text Citations

APA uses the author/date format in the text. Citation of electronic sources should be consistent with this format. If there is no cited author, give the title (or a shortened version if the title is long). If the reference is to a particular part of a text, include the section, page, or chapter number.

The date should be the date of publication. If the source is regularly updated, the date should be that of the most recent update. If date of publication or revision is not known, give the date of your search, indicating that it is the search date and not publication date.

Examples:

Smith, in her FAQ about MUDS, recommends that participants not use the same password for a character on a MUD as the password on their home system accounts because hackers have been known to gain access to MUD files where passwords are maintained (1994, section 3.1).

Or:

A FAQ about MUDS recommends that participants not use the same password for a character on a MUD as the password on their home system accounts because hackers have been known to gain access to MUD files where passwords are maintained (Smith 1994, section 3.1).

2. Reference List

APA uses a reference list instead of a works cited page. APA, as specified in the recent *Publication Manual of the American Psychological Association,* emphasizes including the path information for electronic citations. If publication date is unavailable, use the date you accessed the information.

General Patterns:

Author, I. (date). Title of article. *Name of Periodical* [Online], xx. Available: Specify path

Author, I., & Author, I. (date). Title of chapter. In *Title of full work* [Online]. Available: Specify path

Note: "Specify path" means that you should include the method used to obtain the material, such as Telnet or FTP, the site, and the file name. The patterns are quoted from *Publication Manual of the American Psychological Association* 4th ed. Washington, 1994.

Examples:

About Gopher Jewels (1994). [Online] Available gopher: cwis.usc.edu (128.125.253.145) Directory: /Other Gophers and Information Resources/Gopher–Jewels/Gopher Jewels Information and Help File: About Gopher Jewels.txt

Fanderclai, Tari Lin. MUDs in Education: New Environments, New Pedagogies. *Computer-Mediated Communication Magazine* 2.1 (1995, January 1) [On-line] Available World Wide Web: http://sunsite.unc.edu/cmc/mag/1995/

Smith, Jennifer. Frequently Asked Questions: Basic Information About Muds and Mudding #1. (1994, October 2). [On-line] Available FTP: ftp.univie.ac.at Directory: archive/faq/games/mud-faq/part 1

Smith, Margaret. E-mail to Ann Jones. 20 March 1995.

Wozniak, Adam Peter. Doran's Mudlist. (Accessed 1995, March 14). [On-line] Available E-mail: mudlist@lore.calpoly.edu Message: Mail (in subject line)

SAMPLE STUDENT PAPER UTILIZING INTERNET SOURCES

This paper, written for a first-year composition course, illustrates how you can use the Internet as a research source about controversial topics.

Definition Paper:

Internet Threat

by Alayna Zajic

University of Texas at Austin

Technology today has allowed people to communicate across the world in seconds, gain access to more information than ever before, and express themselves in a free and unique way. The Internet is only one of the new forms of communication, but there has never before been a place to find such vast amounts of information without leaving your desk. USENET newsgroups are an arena where one can read messages posted by other members and communicate about any topic that is of interest with people that have similar interests.

A student of the University of Michigan, Jake Baker, posted on the newsgroup entitled alt.sex.stories a story about kidnapping, raping, and killing a woman. The woman's name and description he used was that of a female student at the university who was in a class with Baker. He was arrested and suspended from school for threatening this woman and sending the story across the global network (Treme). Was this a threat to her? A threat is a direct communication to a specific person that carries the intent of harming that person. Jake Baker's story does not meet all of the criteria, and, therefore, his story is not a case of a threat. Baker never, at any point, directly communicated the story to this woman. A University of Michigan graduate was reading the newsgroup and saw the story; he told the police, who told the university, who told the woman.

The woman was never contacted by Jake Baker himself. He did not call her, send her e-mail, or attempt any other form of communication. Unless he actually presented her with the story, he has done nothing wrong. In the story's prologue Baker specifically states "The premise is that...." He clearly had no intention of carrying out his story in action. Jake had a correspondence with someone by the name of Arthur Gonda. He wrote several messages about child molestation, and when Gonda asked him if he had any intention of doing these things Jake responded, "I have never hurt anyone, and never plan on hurting anyone" (Bebow and Farrell). His statement is not one of someone planning to torture a woman. The simple fact that he wrote a story is not a basis for a threat. Shakespeare wrote about heroes who killed themselves, but he did not end his life. Writers rarely carry out the actions in their works. John Grisham wrote a novel about killing Congressmen. He never intended to actually do this.

Baker's story would qualify as disgusting and sickening by almost anyone's standards, but he is entitled to that perception. There was a definite display of harming someone and taking great pleasure in it, but the plan or intent of action is not there. There was no assault or physical contact. He didn't write her notes or cause her fear in any way. He posted his story in a place meant to have freedom of thought and expression, the Internet. There are currently no laws prohibiting transmissions on the Internet. Baker is currently being held in custody for sending the story across state lines, which has made this a federal issue (Miller). Senator Exon has proposed a bill that would expand the law from telephone lines to all forms of communication on the Internet, or in the telecommunications world (Hayes).

Jake Baker has been compared to a rapist, although he has not committed the act. He is being held to prevent him from doing something that he has not done. This country is based on the freedom of expression and the right to be innocent until proven guilty. Baker has had neither of these privileges. His story is not a silent message of doom to this woman or any woman. Baker wrote a story, period. He did not try to force himself on his fellow student, nor has he had a history of doing so. His intent must have been almost innocent. I cannot say that he does not have a sick mind, or that he did not shame this woman's name, but he did not pose a threat to her. Until he contacted her or made a move towards her, it is a story, a fictional story about a rape and killing.

In conclusion, Jake Baker has not threatened this woman's life or safety. His story is an expression of his thoughts, not a plan of action. I had a dream about killing my roommate. I would never carry out this action, nor would I want her to know that I had thought of this, but it might make an interesting story. If I made it into a story it would be no more an intent than if I kept it to myself. Jake Baker shared his story with people that he believed would enjoy it. Someone felt that it was a threat to this woman's life and it is now jeopardizing the freedom of expression on the Internet.

Works Cited

Bebow, John and Dave Farrell. "Cops Looking for 'Arthur Gonda.'" On-line USENET Newsgroup: alt.sex.stories.d. Internet. 17 Feb. 1995.

Hayes, David. "Protect the Internet." Online. USENET Newsgroup: alt.sex.stories.d. Internet. 17 Feb. 1995.

Miller, Adam S. "The Jake Baker Scandal: Perversion of Logic." On-line. Internet. Accessed 15 March 1995. Available World Wide Web: http://krusty.eecs.umich.edu/people/pjswan/Baker/Jake_Baker.html.

Treme, William B. "Baker Indicted by Grand Jury." Ann Arbor News 15 Feb. 1995 Online. Internet. Accessed 15 March 1995. Available World Wide Web: http://krusty.eecs.umich.edu/people/pjswan/Baker/Arbor.4.

GLOSSARY

anonymous FTP

A service provided by many Internet hosts which does not require any identification or password, allowing any user to transfer documents, files, programs, and other archived data from one computer to another.

Archie

A keyword search system that provides searches for information available via FTP.

archive

A computer that contains a large number of related files.

ASCII

American Standard Code for Information Interchange. Also, in FTP, a text-only file.

binary file

A non-text file such as software or graphics.

Bitnet

One of the major networks that makes up the Internet. Bitnet uses the EBCDIC character set rather than the ASCII character set, and so problems occasionally arise when files are transferred (especially binaries) to and from the Bitnet network. See also FidoNet, UUCPnet.

Boolean operators

Words such as "and," "or," and "not" which are used to logically limit a key-word search. For example, in a database of names, "John and Sam" refers to entries containing both names, while "John not Sam" refers only to those entries that contain the name "John," but do not contain the word "Sam."

browser
A program that enables a person to explore World Wide Web sites by navigating through hypertext links.

bulletin board system (BBS)
A computer configured to provide electronic messaging services, archives of files, and any other services or activities of interest to the bulletin board system's operator.

channel
The basic locations of discussion on IRC. Channels are named with numbers or with strings that begin with a "#" sign followed by topic descriptions which may or may not indicate topics actually discussed on the channel. Once a participant joins a channel, everything he or she types is displayed on the terminals of everyone else currently on that channel.

character
The fictional identity one assumes when using a MUD or MOO.

client/server:
The client/server model is the structure around which many of the Internet protocols are designed. It is a system in which the work is shared between a "host" computer that serves out the information and a "client" computer that receives the information. Client software, be it loaded on your personal computer or accessed on a time-sharing system, handles the tasks of negotiating connections to a remote computer, creating your screen environment, and displaying the information it receives, leaving the server or remote host computer free to perform tasks such as searching a database and sending the results back to you. This model allows client and server software to be developed and maintained separately. This means that several different client software packages can provide access to a particular type of server, so the user can select the client with which he or she is most comfortable. The most widely used client/server protocols are gopher, WAIS, FTP, and the World Wide Web.

commercial provider
An individual or company that provides Internet connectivity for a fee.

directory
A collection of files and subdirectories. Subdirectories are directories within some other directory, known as the parent or root directory.

download
To transfer data from one computer to another. It often refers to transferring to a less powerful or smaller computer. It may also be used to indicate direction, as in "download from"/"upload to."

Ethernet
A 10-megabyte/second local area network developed by Xerox that has become the standard local network protocol.

FidoNet

A worldwide network of personal computers which exchange mail, discussion groups, and files. See also Bitnet, UUCPnet.

File Transfer Protocol (FTP)

A client/server protocol which allows a user on one host to access, and to transfer files to and from, another host over a TCP/IP network.

flame

A message distributed by e-mail, LISTSERV, or USENET intended to insult, provoke, or chastise. Also, as verb, the act of sending such a message.

forum

A term originated by the BBS (bulletin board system) community which refers to a topic-oriented on-line discussion.

free-net

A community computer network which provides free access to local residents.

Frequently asked question (FAQ)

A document created by a system administrator or group moderator to provide answers to common questions for USENET or LISTSERV groups. FAQs are also found at WWW, gopher, and FTP sites to explain content of databases.

gateway

Communications software or protocol that enables data to pass between networks with dissimilar implementations. Also a site that passes data to another network or protocol.

gopherspace

Refers to the gopher sites and documents linked through interconnecting menus.

header

The portion of a packet or message transmitted on the Internet that precedes the actual data. Contains source and destination addresses.

hit

One success in a key-word search via a search engine.

home page

The top-level document or access point for a World Wide Web site. Contains hypertext links to other pages at that site and/or other sites.

host

A computer connected to a network, and thus to the Internet. This computer runs a program that accepts your connections and therefore can be seen as your host. Most host computers are minicomputers and mainframes, but a microcomputer can also act as a host.

host name

The address of a computer on the Internet expressed in letters such as bongo. cc.utexas.edu.

hypertext

A term for a collection of documents containing cross-references or "links" that can be read by a browser program, enabling the user to move easily from one document to another.

Hypertext Markup Language (HTML)

A format used by the World Wide Web pages to indicate typefaces, type size, color, and embedding links in hypertext.

Internet

A collection of networks (including ARPAnet, NSFnet, Milnet, and others) linking universities, commercial sites, private organizations, and military bases around the world.

interrupt character

A key sequence that instructs a computer to stop computation and return control to the user.

IP address

A type of computer address of the form **number.number.number.number** (e.g., **128.170.16.4**). Can be used interchangeably with the host name (e.g., umcvm.umc.edu)

IRC (Internet Relay Chat)

A worldwide "party line" network that allows one to converse with others in real time.

Jughead

A tool that allows keyword searches of local gopher menus. It is an acronym for Jonzy's Universal Gopher Hierarchy Excavation And Display.

keyword search

A method of database searching that looks for certain keywords, or words that describe the topic of the search, specified by the user.

LISTSERV

A discussion group conducted by e-mail. Also a type of program run on some computers in Bitnet that processes electronic mail requests for addition to or deletion from mailing lists.

local area network (LAN)

A network of computers, often within the same building, which are connected in order to share files and printers.

login, logon

The act of getting permission from a computer to use its services. This procedure usually involves telling the computer a user name and corresponding password, so that only authorized people can use a system.

logout, logoff

The act of telling a computer that you are finished and no longer need its services.

mainframe

Term originally referring to the cabinet containing the central processor unit or "main frame" of a room-filling Stone Age batch machine. It now refers to any powerful computer with an interactive time-sharing operating system.

menu-driven

Describes systems protocols that organize data by providing menus. Users can use a mouse or other pointing device to move around easily in directories displayed as menus.

menu tree

Refers to the branching selections offered by a gopher. If you choose one option from the root gopher menu, for example, you receive a new menu of options related to that selection. You follow the branches of a menu tree until you reach the desired information.

mode

The conditions being observed on an IRC channel. May include a password, size limit, access by invitation, and so on.

modem

Acronym for "modulate demodulate." A device that converts digital signals from a computer into analog signals appropriate for transmission over telephone lines (modulate), and converts analog signals into digital signals which a computer can interpret (demodulate).

multi-tasking

A method of utilizing one system to process several different operations at the same time.

MUD

Multi-User Dungeon or Multi-User Dimension. Real-time chat forums with structure; they have multiple "locations" like an adventure game, and may include combat, traps, puzzles, magic, a simple economic system, and the capability for characters to build more structure onto the database that represents the MUD's created world.

netiquette

Network etiquette. Conventions of polite communication on the Internet. Originated in USENET and enforced by peer pressure.

network

A group of computers linked together so they can share data directly with one another.

newsgroup

A USENET discussion group or forum.

news reader

A program that enables a user to read USENET newsgroups.

nick
  The name used to represent a person on IRC, short for nickname. When you connect to IRC, you can use any nick you choose, assuming it is not already allocated to another participant.

node
  See *host.*

operating system
  The software that manages flow, entry, and display of software and data to and from each part of a computer system. The core software that all other software depends on.

packet
  Data transmitted on the Internet is divided into packets which also contain routing information.

PPP
  Point-to-point protocol. The Internet standard for transmission of IP packets over serial (telephone) lines. Allows a user to install software on a personal computer for Internet protocols.

protocol
  A set of agreed-upon rules detailing how to transmit data across a network or between networks. The World Wide Web, for example, has a protocol for transmitting data. Browsers such as Mosaic and Netscape are programs that utilize the protocol.

real-time
  Describes programs or protocols that allow interaction between users within a specified time, usually milliseconds. MUDS and IRC are examples of real-time communication.

RFC (Request For Comment)
  One of a long-established series of numbered Internet informational documents, detailing the protocols upon which the Internet functions.

routing computer
  Processes packets of data and sends them on toward their destination.

routing information
  The information that tells a routing computer where to send a chunk of information.

search engine
  A key-word search site in the World Wide Web.

server
  A program or computer that serves data to another program or computer. See also client.

shell system

An operating system that provides an outer user interface in addition to the kernel of basic services. The shell may offer menu access rather than a naked prompt.

SLIP

Serial Line Internet Protocol. TCP/IP protocols over a serial (telephone) line. SLIP connections, like PPP, allow users to install and run Internet software on personal computers.

sys-op

A term, primarily in reference to bulletin board systems, that refers to the person who maintains a computer system. Also system administrator.

TCP/IP

A protocol suite developed for the Department of Defense and used to allow different types of computers to communicate. Specifies how data packets are sent over networks, including the Internet.

Telnet

A protocol that allows the user to log in to a remote machine connected to the Internet.

terminal

An access point for a remote computer.

terminal emulator

A program that allows a computer to mimic a terminal on a computer system. Used for dial-up access for computer systems.

thread

A topic of conversation in a LISTSERV mailing list or a USENET newsgroup.

time-sharing

An operating system feature allowing users to run several tasks at the same time on one processor.

Universal Resource Locator (URL)

A global address for a resource available on the Internet. URLs were developed as part of and are used extensively by the World Wide Web (WWW) system on the Internet.

UNIX

An interactive time-sharing system invented in 1969 by Ken Thompson, originally so he could play games on his PDP-7 computer. UNIX is ideal for Internet usage because of its uniquely flexible and developer-friendly environment and the fact that it can be used on almost any type of computer.

USENET

Probably the largest decentralized information utility in existence, USENET is a global electronic bulletin board on which millions of people exchange public information on every conceivable topic.

UUCP

An acronym for UNIX-to-UNIX Copy. UUCP is a protocol used by UNIX machines and others to exchange files, typically mail messages and bulletin board articles.

UUCPnet

The store-and-forward network consisting of all the world's connected UNIX machines (and others running some clone of the UUCP (UNIX-to-UNIX Copy) software).

VAX

Digital Equipment Corporation's highly successful minicomputer design.

Veronica

An acronym for Very Easy Rodent-Oriented Net-wide Index to Computerized Archives. Veronica offers a keyword search of most gopher menu titles in the entire gopher web. As Archie is to FTP archives, Veronica is to gopherspace.

VM/CMS

Virtual Machine/Conversational Monitor System. An IBM operating system running on 43XX and 30XX series machines, providing efficient support for large numbers of interactive users.

VMS

DEC's proprietary operating system for its VAX minicomputer.

WAIS

An acronym for Wide Area Information Servers. A distributed document retrieval system supported by Apple, Thinking Machines, and Dow Jones. Servers answer questions from personal workstations following a standard protocol.

Sources of Additional Information

ON-LINE COLLECTIONS ABOUT THE INTERNET

Clearinghouse for Subject-Oriented Internet Resource Guides
    gopher una.hh.lib.umich.edu (/inetdirs)

Computer Networks and Internet Guides (Rice University)
    gopher riceinfo.rice.edu (/Information by Subject Area)

Electronic Frontier Foundation Online Library
    http://www.eff.org

FYI (For Your Information) Documents
    gopher cwis.usc.edu (/Other Gophers and Information/Guides to Internet
    Resources/Documents about Internet Documents

Guides to Internet Resources
    gopher cwis.usc.edu (/Other Gophers and Information Resources/Guides to
    Internet Resources)

Internet Resources
    gopher marvel.loc.gov (/Internet Resources)

Internet Resources Meta Index
    http://www.ncsa.uiuc.edu/SDG/Software/Mosaic/MetaIndex.html

InterNIC (Internet Network Information Center)
    ftp ds.internic.net (/pub/InterNic-info/internic.info)
    or gopher rs.internic.net
    or http://www.internic.net

Merit Network Information Center
  ftp nic.merit.edu
  or gopher nic.merit.edu

Virtual Computer Library
  http://www.utexas.edu/computer/vcl

The Whole Internet Catalog
  http://nearnet.gnn.com/wic/newrescat.toc.html

World Lecture Hall (class materials)
  http://wwwhost.cc.utexas.edu/world/instruction/index.html

World Wide Web Virtual Library
  http://www.w3.org/hypertext/DataSources/DataSources/bySubject

ON-LINE GUIDES TO THE INTERNET

Brown, Alex, Richard Gordon, and Shawn Harvell. *Demystifying the Internet*. 1995.
  Available World Wide Web:
  http:www.udel.edu/eileen/subject/internet/Demyst

Crispen, Patrick Douglas. *Roadmap for the Information Superhighway*. 1995. Available E-mail: LISTSERV@UA1VM.UA.EDU (Command: GET MAIL F=MAIL) *or*
  World Wide Web: http://ua1vm.ua.edu/~crispen/crispen.html

December, John. *Internet Web Text*. 1995. Available World Wide Web:
  http://www.rpi.edu/Internet/Guides/decemj/text.html

Griffin, Adam. *Eff's (Extended) Guide to the Internet*. 1994. Available World Wide
  Web: http://www.eff.org/papers/bdgtti

Introduction to the Internet. University of Michigan School of Information and
  Library Studies. 1995. Available World Wide Web:
  http://www.sils.umich.edu/~fprefect/inet

Kehoe, Brendan. *Zen and the Art of the Internet*. 1992. Available FTP:
  ftp.cs.toronto.edu (/pub/zen)

Kohl, Ed. *Hitchhiker's Guide to the Internet*. 1989. Available gopher:
  cwis.usc.edu (/Other Gophers and Information Resources/Guides to Internet
  Resources)

Kohl, Ed, and E. Koffman. *"What Is the Internet."* 1993. Available gopher:
  cwis.usc.edu (/Gophers and Information Resources/Guides to Internet
  Resources)

Muir, James A. *Browsing the Internet* (for VAX/VMS). 1993. Available gopher:
  gopher.swt.edu (/Computing Services User Manuals)

Sources of Additional Information

Yanoff, Scott. "Yanoff's Special Internet Connection List." 1995. Available World
  Wide Web: http://www.uwm.edu/mirror/inet.services.html

SELECTED INTERNET BOOKS

Bang, Steve, et al. *The Internet Unleashed*. Indianapolis: Sams, 1994.

Braun, Eric. *The Internet Directory*. New York: Fawcett, 1994.

Cronin, Mary. *Doing Business on the Internet*. New York: Van Nostrand, 1994.

Freed, Les and Frank Derfler. *Building the Information Highway*. Emeryville, CA:
  Ziff Davis, 1994.

Gaffin, Adam. *Everybody's Guide to the Internet*. Cambridge: M.I.T. 1994.

Gilster, Paul. *Finding It on the Internet*. New York: Wiley, 1994.

Hahn, Harley, and Rick Stout. *Internet: The Complete Reference*. Berkeley:
  Osborne McGraw-Hill, 1994.

Hoffman, Paul E. *Internet Instant Reference*. Alameda, CA: Sybex, 1994.

Kehoe, Brendan. *Zen & the Art of Internet*. 3rd ed. New York: Prentice Hall, 1994.

Kent, Peter. *The Complete Idiot's Guide to the Internet*. Indianapolis: Alpha, 1994.

Krol, Ed. *The Whole Internet User's Guide and Catalog*. 2nd ed. Cambridge:
  O'Reilly, 1994.

Li, Xia and Nancy Crane. *Electronic Style: A Guide to Citing Electronic Information*.
  Westport, CT: Meckler, 1993.

Miller, Michael. *Easy Internet*. Indianapolis: Que, 1995.

Notess, Greg. *Internet Access Providers: An International Resource Directory*.
  Westport, CT: Meckler, 1994.

Otte, Pete. *The Information Superhighway: Beyond the Internet*. Indianapolis:
  Que, 1994.

Prevost, Ruffin. *Internet Insider*. Berkeley: Osborne McGraw-Hill, 1995.

Rose, Donald. *Minding Your Cybermanners*. Indianapolis: Alpha, 1995.

Sachs, David and Henry Stair. *Hands-On Internet: A Beginning Guide for PC Users*.
  New York: Prentice Hall, 1994.

Tennant, Roy, John Ober, and Anne Lipow. *Crossing the Internet Threshold: An In-
  structional Handbook*. 2nd ed. San Carlos, CA: Library Solutions, 1994.

INDEX

Gopher Jewels, 104–05

host names, 19–20
HTML, 74, 93
hypermedia, 73
hypertext, 73
Hytelnet, 151

Internet connections, 9–13
IRC, 61–4

Jughead, 115

Libraries
    Catalogs, 150, 151
    Library of Congress, 93, 151
    WWW Virtual Library, 94
List Global, 36
LISTSERV, 31–46
    groups, 42–5
    Command Job Language, Interpreter, 37
local area network, 10
Lynx, 83–90

MLA, 165–66
MOO, 64–9
Mosaic, 75
MUD, 64–9
mudder, 64
museums, 94

netiquette, 35–6, 54–5
Netscape, 75, 78–83
newspapers, 94
nick, 62
No News, 56

packets, 5
Pine, 22–26
PPP, 10, 13
Prodigy, 11

Project Gutenberg, 118–37

Read News (rn), 56
research, 160–62
root gopher, 97–8

search engines, 90–3
signatures, 18
SLIP, 10, 13
smilies, 18
sports, 94
subscribing (LISTSERV), 32

TALK, 58–9
TCP/IP, 5
Telnet, 144–51
terminal emulator, 9, 12, 145
threads, 54
Threaded Read News (trn), 56
time-sharing, 9
TN3270, 145
Turbogopher, 105–8

UNIX, 10
UNIX FTP, 131–37
URL, 76
USENET newsgroups, 47–57
UUCP, 47

Veronica, 112–15
VMS, 10

WAIS, 152–59
World Wide Web, 73–95
    graphical browser, 78–83
    Lynx, 83–90
    pages, 74
    search engines, 90–3
WebCrawler, 90–3
White House, 78–83